ENDORS

The death of Jesus for our sins is the heart of the Christian faith. What does a physician have to say about that death? That's the subject of this important new book, examining the medical evidence from the Biblical texts. Particularly intriguing are the details of the death of Jesus as found in the *Old* Testament, written hundreds of years before the actual event.

—Jerry Newcombe, D.MIN.
TV Producer, Ft. Lauderdale, Florida
Co-author of numerous books with D. James Kennedy, PH.D.,
including *Christ's Passion: The Power and the Promise*

In this complete treatment of the crucifixion and the suffering associated with this kind of punishment, Dr. Marinella reminds us of "man's inhumanity to man" and God's great love for us to accept this form of death to provide such a great salvation.

—Jonathan M. Saxe, M.D., F.A.C.S.
Professor of Surgery
Director of Trauma Research, Wright State University
Candidate Master of Arts in Religious Studies
Liberty University, Lynchburg, Virginia

It takes a physician to pronounce a man dead. It takes a student to research how and why a man dies. Mark is both! As a physician of medicine and a student of the Bible, Mark has not only discovered that a man died, he has also learned why He died. The man—Jesus! The reason—we need a Savior!

—David K. Smith, D.D.
Christian & Missionary Alliance Board
Senior Pastor, Fairhaven Church, Dayton, Ohio

Dr. Marinella's bedside manner displays his depth of scientific understanding, but also his compassion. His study of the Cross will deepen your faith.

—Dennis M. Sullivan, M.D., M.A. (Ethics)
Professor of Biology, Director, Center for Bioethics
Cedarville University, Cedarville, Ohio

DIED HE FOR ME

A PHYSICIAN'S VIEW
OF THE CRUCIFIXION
OF JESUS CHRIST

DIED HE FOR ME

A PHYSICIAN'S VIEW
OF THE CRUCIFIXION
OF JESUS CHRIST

Mark A. Marinella, M.D., F.A.C.P.

Nordskog Publishing inc.

Ventura, California

2008

Died He for Me:
A Physician's View of the Crucifixion of Jesus Christ

published by

 Nordskog
Publishing Inc.

© 2008 by Mark A. Marinella, M.D., F.A.C.P.

International Standard Book Number: 978-0-9796736-6-5

Library of Congress Control Number: 2008940821

Unless otherwise indicated, all Scripture quotations are from:
The Holy Bible, New International Version®
Copyright ©1973, 1978, 1984 International Bible Society. All rights reserved
throughout the world. Used by permission of International Bible Society.
[Initial caps have been added to pronouns referring to the LORD.]

"The Post Resurrection Appearances of Jesus,"
"Footsteps of Jesus during His Last Days," and
"Jesus' Hours upon the Cross," on pp. xviii, 60, & 68.
Taken from the Thompson® Chain-Reference® Bible.
Used with permission of Kirkbride Bible Company.

Book Cover Design by Robbie Destocki
(creativeimagedesigngroup@yahoo.com)

Editor & Interior Design, Desta Garrett
(DG Ink Book Design, info@dg-ink.net)

Theology Editor, Ronald Kirk

Proofreader, Kimberley Winters

Theological Analysis of Manuscript, Rev. Christopher Hoops

Manuscript Edit, Mark A. Kakkuri
(Oxford, MI, kakkuri@gmail.com)

Printed in the United States of America.

NORDSKOG PUBLISHING, INC.
2716 Sailor Ave., Ventura, California 93001 USA
1-805-642-2070 • 1-805-276-5129
www.NordskogPublishing.com

Christian Small Publishers Association

TABLE OF CONTENTS

LIGHT AND THE LAW
by Arnold Friberg

PREFACE

THE CRUX OF CHRISTIANITY

*He Himself bore our sins in
His body on the tree,
so that we might die to sins and
live for righteousness;
by His wounds you have been healed.*

(1 Peter 2:24)

THE *crux* of Christianity is salvation through faith that Jesus Christ is God in the flesh, that He died on the cross, that He rose again to life in bodily form, and now sits at God the Father's right hand. None of us deserves eternal bliss, but in His overwhelming love for mankind, God came to earth in human flesh as the God-man, Jesus Christ, and gave His life freely, securing our salvation through faith.

Christians celebrate Christ's resurrection each spring, the pinnacle of our Christian calendar we call "Easter." Without Christ's necessary, yet voluntary, gruesome death during Passover week, none of us would have the hope and promise of salvation.

I have often found fellow believers uncomfortable when it comes to discussing Jesus' sacrifice, especially the graphic details of the flogging or the crucifixion. However, we as frail human beings need to comprehend and appreciate Jesus' voluntary sacrifice and suffering made for all generations. The goal of this book is not to affix blame as to who killed Jesus. Indeed,

I am just as responsible as anyone involved during the trials and execution, since it is also my sin that nailed Him to the cross. In fact, contemplating my own sin and its effects have made me painfully more aware of the value of the tremendous sacrifice Jesus made to restore me to His grace. Brennan Manning sums up Christ's mind-boggling sacrifice for our sin:

> The unconditional love of Jesus Christ nailed to the wood does not flinch before the worst sinner's perversity and inhumanity (*A Glimpse of Jesus*, 2003, 91).

As a Christian physician, I have not only marveled at the spiritual ramifications of Christ's death, but also at the physical and physiological aspects. For instance, Pilate's flogging of Jesus probably left Him in critical condition due to massive blood loss, tissue injury, and great distress. Based on the physical response to the severe beatings, lack of food and sleep, and great spiritual anguish, I believe Jesus' body was in shock and already nearing death as He was nailed to the cross. To present this, I have compiled a succinct overview of Jesus' death from a physical and medical perspective that, I hope, both lay and medical people can appreciate and understand.

My desire is that when we contemplate the crucifixion so often casually taken for granted, we will not forget the physical suffering and sacrifice Christ underwent in a purely voluntary manner, simply because of His love for each one of us. We need to digest and understand that "Jesus was a naked, humiliated, exposed God on the cross who allowed us to get close to Him" (Manning, 137), and that He would have died for each of us, even if we were the only person to ever live.

Mark A. Marinella, M.D., F.A.C.P.
Dayton, Ohio, November 2008

This book is dedicated
to my daughters,
Elise and Lauren—

God has truly blessed me
beyond measure.

FOREWORD

IN *Died He for Me: A Physician's View of the Crucifixion of Jesus Christ*, Mark Marinella, M.D. eloquently guides readers through the physiologic process that was occurring in Jesus' body over His final few hours, while also providing a historical background on crucifixion as a method of execution. This book is also written for non-physicians, providing medical and scientific knowledge in an understandable and insightful manner.

Dr. Marinella examines Old Testament prophecy as it relates to the crucifixion, informing the reader of subtle points that are actually important. For example, Deuteronomy 21:22-23 states,

> If a man guilty of a capital offense is put to death and his body is hung on a tree, you must not leave his body on the tree overnight. Be sure to bury him that same day, because anyone who is hung on a tree is under God's curse. You must not desecrate the land the LORD your God is giving you as an inheritance.

Christ was removed from the cross and buried before sundown:

> Now it was the day of Preparation, and the next day was to be a special Sabbath. Because the Jews did not want the bodies left on the crosses during the Sabbath, they asked Pilate to have the legs broken and the bodies taken down (John 19:31).

However, as Christ was already dead, Pilate did not have His legs broken, fulfilling prophecy in the Exodus 12:46 instruction for handling the Passover lamb: "...do not break any of the bones."

The in-depth evaluation of the crucifixion of Christ is humbling and will likely lead believers and unbelievers to have even more respect and admiration for the God who provided this salvation.

Dr. Marinella's experience as a physician enables him to review the Bible and comment from a modern standpoint on the medical conditions that Christ was likely to have experienced in His final hours on earth before He miraculously rose from the dead on the third day.

Christ died as atonement for sins. Medical knowledge of human physiology was very limited in the time of Christ. *Died He for Me* will help readers understand what Christ likely went through physically and spiritually to sacrifice His life for our sins so that Christians can spend eternity with our LORD. Obviously, at the time of Christ routine laboratory studies or *radiographic imaging* could not be performed, so Dr. Marinella's ideas are based on expert opinion and cannot be backed up by medical evidence. However, the conclusions drawn by him are plausible and are excellent explanations of what physiologic processes were likely occurring in Christ during His final hours.

As a believer, I am humbled at the price that was paid and trust you will be too. If you are a non-Christian or unbeliever, you will have the opportunity to understand an aspect of the depth of love that Christ displayed on the cross.

All human religious icons have died, but only One rose to life again. And Dr. Marinella's book helps us to realize what Jesus suffered in His willing and voluntary experience of the total destruction of His physical body during His torture, and that there is no doubt He did truly die, and yet that He subsequently rose to life again from the dead. Through this in-depth "sharing in His sufferings," we come to ever more appreciate this awesome display of love and power by our LORD.

To God be the glory!

Steven D. Burdette, M.D.
Assistant Professor of Internal Medicine
Wright State University School of Medicine, Dayton, Ohio

THE PUBLISHER'S WORD

My God, My God, why have You forsaken Me?
(Mark 15:34, Psalm 22:1a)

As horrific as the physical torture and murder of the King of kings and Lord of lords was, the abandonment and forsakenness (spiritual separation) of the Son from the Father as our Savior bore and atoned all of the sins of the world was the crowning moment of this pinnacle event that has separated time in *His Story* (history). As the author states at the conclusion of chapter 6, "Jesus felt upon His shoulders the weight of all the sin of fallen mankind and the wrath of His Holy Father...."

When the Rev. Christopher Hoops and I first discussed the potential of publishing Dr. Mark Marinella's book, our initial thought was that it is more important to emphasize the Doctrine of Redemption rather than primarily the physical aspects of the Savior's passion week of torture and death. But it is impossible to separate one from the other. The incarnate Jesus (fully man and fully God) purposed more than 2000 years ago to fulfill His role on earth and voluntarily submit to suffer, die, and take upon Himself the sins of the entire world.

According to Dr. D. James Kennedy and Dr. Jerry Newcombe,

> In the Gospels, one-third of Matthew, Mark, and Luke deal with Christ's sufferings and death. One-half of John's Gospel deals with the last week of Jesus' life. The Apostles' Creed, which affirms facts about Christ's life, takes a tremendous leap from the birth of Christ to His suffering and death. It passes over His entire ministry. The Creed says nothing about Jesus' great teachings, about His marvelous example, or about the incredible miracles He performed. The focus of all these works communicates the tremendous importance of Christ's suffering and pain.*

---

* Kennedy, D. James, Ph.D. and Jerry Newcombe, D.Min., *New Every Morning* (March 21). Portland, OR: Multnomah Books, 1996.

Faninus, a learned layman who was martyred in 1550 in Italy for his faith, said this on his execution day:

> Christ sustained all manner of pangs and conflicts, with hell and death, on our accounts; and thus by His sufferings, freed those who really believe in Him from the fear of them. (www.exclassics.com/foxe/foxe161.htm)

Because of God's holiness, humankind's sin, God's justice, and God's love, Jesus voluntarily endured the cross to save those (take the punishment deserved by humans) who would believe in Him (Matthew 26:39):

> Going a little farther, He fell with His face to the ground and prayed, "My Father, if it is possible, may this cup be taken from Me. Yet not as I will, but as You will."

The cup contained all the sin of the world. Christ took it in obedience, this bitter cup of God's abandonment and wrath against sin. He is perfect and holy, voluntarily laying down His own life, taking *our deserved punishment*, in both a physical and spiritual death (separation from God, the Father), this for all the sins of mankind, past, present, and future, for those who believed and will believe in the atonement of Christ, and are imputed Christ's righteousness. Our Savior victoriously conquered death as He rose from the grave.

This was the Passion of Jesus Christ. The word *passion* comes from a Latin word meaning "to submit to suffering." Jesus was mocked and ridiculed, spat upon, beaten with fists and whips, His back ripped to ribbons, His brow bruised and bloody from the crown of thorns pressed into His flesh, nailed to a cross and condemned to a most brutal and agonizing death, physically and spiritually. All for us.

> I love Thee, because Thou has first loved me,
>   and purchased my pardon on Calvary's tree.
> I love Thee for wearing the thorns on Thy brow;
>   if ever I loved Thee, My Jesus 'tis now.
>   —William R. Featherstone

> Therefore, there is now no condemnation for those who are in Christ Jesus, because through Christ Jesus the law of the Spirit of life set me free from the law of sin and death. For what the Law was powerless to do in that it was weakened by the sinful nature, God did by sending His own Son in the likeness of sinful man to be a sin offering. And so He condemned sin in sinful man, in order that the righteous requirements of the law might be fully met in us, who do not live according to the sinful nature but according to the Spirit. (Romans 8:1-4)

To believe in Christ means to accept Him as Lord and Master of our lives. Napoleon in his latter days at St. Helena is alleged to have said,

> Across a chasm of eighteen hundred years, Christ makes a demand which is above all others difficult to satisfy. He asks for that which a philosopher may often seek at the hands of his friends, or a father of his children, or a bride of her spouse. He asks for the human heart, for His very own, exclusively His. Wonderful! In defiance of time and space, the soul of man with all its powers becomes an annexation to the Empire of Christ.*

After the Resurrection from the grave by Christ on the third day after His burial in a sealed tomb, for forty days our Lord made post-resurrection appearances to hundreds of people on earth before His ascension to heaven to the right hand of the Father and where He makes constant intercession for His people (those who love Him). Please look up these Scripture passages, in which Jesus assured His followers that He was alive in a glorified body (and could be touched and felt, eat food [fish], and still revealed the scars from His ordeal on the cross). And He is alive today and forevermore.

> A week later His disciples were in the house again, and Thomas with them. Though the doors were locked, Jesus

---

* Kennedy, D. James, Ph.D. and Jerry Newcombe, D.Min., *New Every Morning* (August 17). Portland, OR: Multnomah Books, 1996.

came and stood among them and said, "Peace be with you!"
Then He said to Thomas, "Put your finger here; see my
hands. Reach out your hand and put it into my side. Stop
doubting and believe." Thomas said to Him, "My Lord and
my God!" Then Jesus told him, "Because you have seen me,
you have believed; blessed are those who have not seen and
yet have believed."   (John 20:26-29)

The Post-Resurrection Appearances of Jesus*

Easter (Resurrection) Day:
> Mary Magdalene (Mark 16:9), Other women (Matthew 28:9),
> Peter (1 Corinthians 15:5), Jerusalem; Two disciples (Luke 24:15-31),
> Emmaus; Ten apostles, Thomas absent (John 20:19), Jerusalem.

Sunday following the Resurrection:
> Eleven disciples, Thomas present (John 20:26-29), Jerusalem.

Time unknown:
> Seven disciples fishing (John 21:1-24),
> Jesus' charge to Peter (John 21:15-17), Sea of Galilee;
> Eleven disciples (Matthew 28:16-17),
> Five hundred brethren (1 Corinthians 15:6),
> James (1 Corinthians 15:7), Two disciples (Mark 16:12),
> Eleven disciples (Acts 1:2-9), places unknown.

Ascension Day:
> Eleven disciples (Matthew 28:16-20), mountain in Galilee;
> (Mark 16:14-20); (Luke 24:50-52), Bethany.

Later Appearance (time unknown):
> Saul/Paul (Acts 9:1-6, 1 Corinthians 15:8), road to Damascus.

And here is the last commission of Jesus to His eleven disciples
(Galilee mountainside) and for all of His followers, the true
Church, the Bride of Christ forevermore:

> Then Jesus came to them and said, "All authority in heaven
> and on earth has been given to me. Therefore go and make

---

* In part from the Thompson Chain Reference® Bible, Kirkbride Bible Company.
The Gospel records of these appearances are somewhat obscure.
Scholars differ in their opinions as to their exact number and order.

disciples of all nations, baptizing them in the name of the Father and of the Son and of the Holy Spirit, and teaching them to obey everything I have commanded you. And surely I am with you always, to the very end of the age."

(Matthew 28:18-20)

This is our duty, our commission from our Master. We are also to remember Him and honor Him by regularly taking of the Lord's Supper, Holy Communion, together with other believers in the faith.

"...do this, whenever you drink it, in remembrance of Me." For whenever you eat this bread and drink this cup, you proclaim the Lord's death until He comes.

(1 Corinthians 11:24b, 26)

While they were eating, Jesus took bread, gave thanks and broke it, and gave it to His disciples, saying, "Take and eat; this is My body." Then He took the cup, gave thanks and offered it to them, saying, "Drink from it, all of you. This is my blood of the [new] covenant, which is poured out for many for the forgiveness of sins. I tell you, I will not drink of this fruit of the vine from now on until that day when I drink it anew with you in My Father's kingdom."

(Matthew 26:26-29)

He said to me: "It is done. I am the Alpha and the Omega, the Beginning and the End. To him who is thirsty I will give to drink without cost from the spring of the water of life. He who overcomes will inherit all this, and I will be his God and he will be My son." (Revelation 21:6-7)

We are pleased to be publishing Dr. Mark Marinella's inspiring book.

— Gerald Christian Nordskog
Thanksgiving 2008

INTRODUCTION

*I want to know Christ
and the power of His resurrection
and the fellowship of sharing in His sufferings,
becoming like Him in His death, and so, somehow
to attain to the resurrection from the dead.*
(Philippians 3:10-11)

THIS study detailing a medical interpretation of the physical aspects of the crucifixion has also been framed in the understanding of Christ's incarnation, spiritual suffering, and humiliation. The crucifixion and resurrection of Christ provides the focal point for studying the life of Christ—and the life of the King of kings is marked by a paradoxical humiliation.

Philippians 2 provides the context for understanding the sum of His life, death, and resurrection.

> Your attitude [mind] should be the same as that of Christ Jesus:
>
> Who, being in the very nature God, did not consider equality with God something to be grasped, but made Himself nothing, taking the very nature of a servant, being made in human likeness. And being found in appearance as a man, He humbled Himself and became obedient to death—even death on a cross!
>
> Therefore God exalted Him to the highest place and gave Him the name that is above every name, that at

the name of Jesus every knee should bow, in heaven and on earth and under the earth, and every tongue confess that Jesus Christ is Lord, to the glory of God the Father.   (Philippians 2:5-11)

Christ did not take advantage of His Godhood. Not only did He set aside His heavenly powers and come to earth in human form, He was also fully God and fully man while on earth. Consider the heavenly power that was available to Christ through each facet of the trial and crucifixion. He had choice and the power to stop them at any time or just slip away, as in Luke 4:30.

He came as a baby under humiliating circumstances. Christ experienced growing up and learning: "And Jesus increased in wisdom and in stature and in favor with God and man" (Luke 2:52). He lived thirty-three years in perfect righteousness, and that obedience and fulfillment of the law, as well as His death and sacrifice, were needed for our forgiveness and salvation.

See Isaiah 53 (quoted in full on page 10). Jesus is the epitome of the humble, suffering servant and a perfect example for His followers. Christ's humility started with becoming human, being obedient, being willing to die, and culminated in death on a cross, the most humiliating torture ever conceived. In addition to the extended physical pain, a crucifixion was also a public spectacle marked by mocking, insults, jeering, and nakedness. The Apostle Paul emphasized Christ's humiliation, not His physical suffering, and points out that the same humility that compelled Christ to the cross should inform Christians how they should conduct themselves toward others.

Jesus Christ paid the ultimate price to provide eternal salvation to those who believe in Him—He gave His life as atonement for sins. Christ, being God incarnate, could have chosen other means to provide our salvation and chosen another process to give His life as a sacrifice. Jesus Christ was tortured beyond belief, suffered an agonizing death, and was buried, fulfilling the Scriptures. At the height of His suffering, "He did not open His mouth" (Isaiah 53:7b) to complain or condemn, but to pray for those who were torturing Him, "Father, forgive them, for they do not know what they are doing" (Luke 23:34a).

Although this book examines in detail from a twenty-first-century medical-science perspective the torture and trauma done to Jesus and the multifaceted physiological processes involved in the total destruction of His physical human body, proving He was actually dead and not just unconscious when placed in the tomb, in the final analysis, no one can claim to prove a physical cause of death. These details were part of the predetermined plan for sinners to be reconciled to the Holy God. And now God calls all men everywhere to repent (Acts 17:30) and put their trust in Christ's atoning work on the cross.

John stated (3:19), "This is the verdict: Light has come into the world, but men loved darkness instead of light because their deeds were evil." The providential cause and timing of Jesus' death are revealed in the Word and spiritually discerned: that although man cannot save himself,

> God so loved the world that He gave His one and only Son, that whoever believes in Him shall not perish but have eternal life (John 3:16).

The sins of mankind have been atoned for by Christ's death and those who trust in Christ alone will have everlasting life.

— EDITOR

ISAIAH 53

¹Who has believed our message and to whom has the arm of the Lord been revealed? ²He grew up before Him like a tender shoot, and like a root out of dry ground. He had no beauty or majesty to attract us to Him, nothing in His appearance that we should desire Him. ³He was despised and rejected by men, a man of sorrows, and familiar with suffering. Like one from whom men hide their faces He was despised and, we esteemed Him not.

⁴Surely He took up our infirmities and carried our sorrows, yet we considered Him stricken by God, smitten by Him, and afflicted. ⁵But He was pierced for our transgressions, He was crushed for our iniquities; the punishment that brought us peace was upon Him, and by His wounds we are healed. ⁶We all, like sheep, have gone astray, each of us has turned to his own way; and the Lord has laid upon Him the iniquity of us all. ⁷He was oppressed and afflicted, yet He did not open His mouth; He was led like a lamb to the slaughter, and as a sheep before her shearers is silent, so He did not open His mouth. ⁸By oppression and judgment He was taken away. And who can speak of His descendants? For He was cut off from the land of the living; for the transgression of My people He was stricken. ⁹He was assigned a grave with the wicked, and with the rich in His death, though He had done no violence, nor was any deceit in His mouth.

¹⁰Yet it was the Lord's will to crush Him and cause Him to suffer, and though the Lord makes His life a guilt offering, He will see His offspring and prolong His days, and the will of the Lord will prosper in His hand. ¹¹After the suffering of His soul, He will see the light of life and be satisfied; by His knowledge My righteous servant will justify many, and He will bear their iniquities. ¹²Therefore I will give Him a portion among the great, and He will divide the spoils with the strong, because He poured out His life unto death, and was numbered with the transgressors. For He bore the sin of many and made intercession for the transgressors. *[Initial caps added to pronouns referring to the Lord.]*

1

WHAT THE
OLD TESTAMENT
SAYS

Then Moses summoned all the elders
of Israel and said to them,
"Go at once and select the animals
for your families and
slaughter the Passover lamb."
(Exodus 12:21)

T HE prediction of Christ's death appears numerous times in the Old Testament, and the New Testament necessarily stands in the context of the Old. Together the testaments provide an amazing discourse of history and prophecy with regard to Christ's crucifixion and resurrection, giving historical credence to the story of what the followers of Jesus Christ call the Gospel.

GENESIS

Genesis holds so much history and promise that it is impossible in a short work like this to cover all of the deep theological and prophetic issues relating to the New Testament. However, some of the more pertinent and obvious references to Christ's coming sacrifice are worth noting. The earliest reference to Christ in the Bible comes in Genesis 3:15, God's curse upon the serpent after deceiving Adam and Eve: "And I will put enmity between you and the woman, and between your offspring and hers; He will crush your head, and you will strike His heel." The offspring of the woman includes humanity and, ultimately, Jesus' followers. As such, Satan and his followers would try to cripple mankind by crucifying Christ ("strike His heel"), but ultimately Christ would deliver the final, fatal blow to evil by His resurrection ("He will crush your head"). This means that in order for Him to emerge victorious over Satan, Christ must offer Himself in sacrifice—to suffer the reality of death on a cross. The cross would prove to be horrid and painful but, as we shall see in later chapters, necessary.

Perhaps the greatest foreshadowing in Scripture of Christ's sacrificial death is found in Genesis chapter 22, the story of Abraham and Isaac. God promised Abraham and Sarah a son in their old age. That son was Isaac, whom God asked Abraham to sacrifice with the knife and fire on Mount Moriah. Abraham was obedient and led Isaac, who carried the wood for the fire on his own back, on the long journey to the mountain: "Abraham took the wood for the burnt offering and placed it on his son Isaac" (Genesis 22:6). This verse parallels Christ's carrying of the "wood" cross upon His shoulders to His own sacrifice, but there was no animal sacrifice to save Him as there ultimately was for Isaac. Abraham in his obedient spirit was about to slay his son when God provided a sacrificial ram in the thicket that served as a substitute for Isaac (Genesis 22:13). Abraham prophesied in verse 8, "God Himself will provide the lamb...." This provision clearly promised that God would provide our sacrificial lamb, Jesus Christ, as in John 1:29:

> The Lamb of God,
> Who takes away the sin of the world.

EXODUS

Exodus foreshadows Christ's sacrificial death in the experience of the Passover, which the Jews have celebrated ever since to commemorate their release from Egyptian captivity. In addition,

Exodus 6:6 may suggest the type of death the Messiah would later suffer for mankind's redemption: "I will redeem you with an outstretched arm...." Christ literally stretched out His arms upon the cross and nails were driven into His wrists—all for our salvation and redemption. Although this verse refers to God figuratively stretching out His arm to lead the children of Israel out of Egyptian bondage, it may also suggest the horrific death that Jesus would suffer thousands of years later.

Filled with symbolism, Passover is observed annually and much of the celebration centers upon a meal, as with Christ's Last Supper, the last Passover He shared with the disciples. An amazing aspect of the first Passover was God's command for each family to sacrifice an unblemished lamb (representing the sinless Jesus) and smearing the blood of the lamb on the door-frame of the family's home. The presence of the blood on the doorframe led to the death angel "passing over" the dwelling, with all inhabitants escaping the destructive plague of death that affected every Egyptian household (Exodus 12). In similar fashion, Christ's shedding of His blood on the wood frame of the cross provides escape from eternal death for those who trust in His saving grace. The blood of the lamb (in Exodus) and the Lamb (in the Gospels) seeped into the wood and stained it, leaving a visible reminder of the need for a blood sacrifice for atonement of sin.

With regard to the Passover lamb, Exodus 12:46 states: "do not break any of the bones." Moses reiterated the command to the Jews about their annual Passover lamb in Numbers 9:12: "They must not...break any of its bones." These verses foreshadow that Christ died without His bones being broken, fulfilling these verses in Exodus and Numbers and, as we shall see, also a passage in Psalm 34.

LEVITICUS

Throughout Leviticus, the priestly duties regarding the slaughter and sacrifice of animals to atone for the Israelites' sin are described in painstaking detail. Of greatest significance is the annual Atonement, a day of great fasting when the high priest entered the Most Holy Place in the Tabernacle with the blood of the sacrifice to reconcile the people with God by atoning for their sins. The priest, going behind the curtain, sought God's forgiveness for the people:

> He shall then slaughter the goat for the sin offering for the people and take its blood behind the curtain.... He shall sprinkle it on the atonement cover and in front of it. In this way he will make atonement...because of the uncleanness and rebellion of the Israelites, whatever their sins have been (Leviticus 16:15–16).

Blood is a vital component of redemption under the old as well as the new covenant. Leviticus 17:11 states:

> For the life of a creature is in the blood, and I have given it to you to make atonement for yourselves...; it is the blood that makes atonement for one's life.
>
> [And]...without the shedding of blood there is no forgiveness (Hebrews 9:22b).

As the Hebrew writer points out to us, this foreshadowed Christ's substitutionary death once and for all when He was crucified millennia later:

> Nor did He enter heaven to offer Himself again and again, the way the high priest enters the Most Holy Place every year with blood that is not his own (Hebrews 9:25).

When Christ died, "The curtain of the temple was torn in two, from top to bottom" (Mark 15:38). Consequently, God is no longer "veiled" behind the curtain, and we can now enter into His direct presence through the atoning death and sacrifice of His Son, Jesus. Paul summarizes this concept in 2 Corinthians 3:16: "But whenever anyone turns to the Lord, the veil is taken away." We do not need a priest to repetitively enter the previously forbidden Most Holy Place where the presence of God dwelt. Instead, Christ opened the door for our direct access to God,

> once for all...to do away with sin by the sacrifice of Himself (Hebrews 9:26b).

NUMBERS

Many may find the book of Numbers a daunting challenge to read, since this book is filled with the census tables of the Israelites and dense historical dissertation. However, it reveals some important prophecy. Numbers 21 describes an incident when God sent deadly venomous snakes to bite the Israelites for complaining bitterly against Him and Moses. Many people died, which pushed them, as in previous predicaments, to confession. Moses interceded for the Israelites, petitioning God to remove the snakes and save the people from the deadly venom. God in His abundant mercy and grace responded by instructing Moses how to provide a way to escape death if they had faith and believed:

> So Moses prayed for the people. The Lord said to Moses, "Make a snake and put it up on a pole; anyone who is bitten can look at it and live." So Moses made a bronze snake and put it up on a pole. Then when anyone was bitten by a snake and looked at the bronze snake, he lived (Numbers 21:7-9).

This portion of Scripture unquestionably prophesies the crucifixion, or "lifting up" of the Son of Man bearing our sin on a wooden cross or pole. During the famous discussion with Nicodemus, Jesus said,

> Just as Moses lifted up the snake in the desert, so the Son of Man must be lifted up, that everyone who believes in Him may have eternal life (John 3:14-15).

Likewise, John quoting Jesus' own words, said,

> "But I, when I am lifted up from the earth, will draw all men to Myself." He said this to show the kind of death He was going to die (John 12:32-33).

Clearly, if we believe with sincere faith that Christ was "lifted up" and subsequently died and rose again for our sins, we like the Israelites may be saved from death if we "look up" at Christ bearing our sin on the pole.

DEUTERONOMY

Perhaps the most vivid allusion to crucifixion made during Mosaic times is found in Deuteronomy 21:22-23:

> If a man guilty of a capital offense is put to death and his body is hung on a tree, you must not leave his body on the tree overnight. Be sure to bury him that same day, because anyone who is hung on a tree is under God's curse.

During the Exodus and preceding their settling into the promised land, God gave Moses decrees and commands for the Israelites to follow in order to maintain an orderly, God-centered society. Criminals who were executed were often hung on a tree after death to deter others from committing the same offense. However, the dead body was not to be left hanging on the tree overnight, much in the same way that bodies that were crucified on the eve of a Sabbath needed to be removed before sunset. Jesus was cursed by man and God to absorb all past, present, and future sin and hung on a wooden cross for all to see. Paul points out this curse in Galatians 3:13:

> Christ redeemed us from the curse of the law by becoming a curse for us, for it is written: "Cursed is everyone who is hung on a tree."

THE PSALMS

Some of the most dramatic highlights of Scripture relevant to Christ's crucifixion are found in the Psalms, especially those that predict His physical torment and death. The Psalms and passages in the writings of the Prophets have some of the most obvious and dramatic prophecies regarding Jesus' physical suffering, which would not occur for several hundred years.

There are several Messianic Psalms that portray Christ as the coming Messiah out of the line of David. This work discusses only a sample of those psalms which prophesy and predict the crucifixion and physical torture of Jesus of Nazareth. Psalm 16 shows King David's confidence in God in the midst of any trouble, and he had many. David knew that God would deliver him through any adversity; he attests to this in verse 8: "Because He is at my right hand, I will not be shaken." He knew that after death he would see God according to his faith that resulted in his salvation: "my body will also rest secure" (verse 9). However, Psalm 16 takes on a prophetic tone in verse 10: "because You will not abandon Me to the grave, nor will You let Your Holy One see decay." Clearly, King David did not mean this verse to apply to himself since he was a mortal man whose body would decompose after death. This prophetically points to the bodily resurrection of Jesus without decay. In Acts 2, the Apostle Peter quoted this psalm to the assembled crowd. Peter goes on to say in Acts 2:30-31:

But he [David] was a prophet and knew that God had promised him on oath that He would place one of his descendants on his throne. Seeing what was ahead, he spoke of the resurrection of the Christ, that He was not abandoned to the grave, nor did His body see decay.

Psalm 22 may be the most well-known of the Messianic Psalms that foreshadow Christ's suffering and death. Charles Spurgeon called this "...beyond all others 'The Psalm of the Cross'".[38] Some scholars suggest that Jesus may have recited the whole psalm while He hung on the cross, but the best-known quote by Jesus from this psalm is found in verse one:

"My God, My God, why have You forsaken Me?"

This is one of Jesus' seven recorded utterances from the cross, and yet possibly the most revealing of His temporary separation from His Father who turned His back upon His own Son—because how can a holy God look upon sin. David is clearly remembered as a godly king, but in several of the psalms, especially Psalm 22, we see David as a prophet, like Isaiah or Jeremiah.

Although Psalm 22 applies to David's earthly afflictions, the examples prophesying Christ's death are clearly seen as well. For instance, verses 7 and 8 state:

All who see Me mock Me; they hurl insults, shaking their heads: "He trusts in the LORD; let the LORD rescue Him. Let Him [the LORD] deliver Him, since He delights in Him."

These words are very similar to the way the chief priests, the teachers of the law, and the elders mocked Him as the Gospel of Matthew records in 27:39-41:

Those who passed by hurled insults at Him, shaking their heads and saying, "You who are going to destroy the temple and build it in three days, save yourself! Come down from the cross, if you are the Son of God!"

Mark's version is very similar (15:31b):

"He saved others," they said, "but He can't save Himself."

In Psalm 22:14 David says:

I am poured out like water, and all My bones are out of joint. My heart has turned to wax; it has melted away within Me.

Jesus was exhausted, "poured out like water" from sleep deprivation, intense stress, sweating in the hot Middle East sun, and the injuries from His flogging. He literally poured out volumes of water in the form of sweat and through the lungs in the form of water vapor. His bones literally were out of joint due to the tremendous forces applied to the skeleton when hanging on a cross. "My heart has turned to wax" is figurative pertaining to His exhaustion and physical collapse. However, in Christ's critical medical condition, His heart literally was likely beginning to fail and becoming *hypokinetic*, or dilated, and beating weakly. This is not unlike the change in form that occurs as wax is heated and starts to melt. Psalm 22 goes on:

My strength is dried up like a potsherd, and My tongue sticks to the roof of My mouth (v. 15).

These graphic details describe a man in a physically weakened condition who has lost significant amounts of bodily fluids and become dehydrated. By the time Jesus was on the cross, He had already been without food or drink, had lost hydration through sweating in the arid climate, and had likely lost large amounts of blood from the wounds inflicted at His scourging.

David further states (in verse 16b):

…they have pierced My hands and My feet.

This refers to the piercing of Christ's hands and feet with long spikes as He was nailed to the cross. The pain of this act is unthinkable. Jesus was likely crucified in a loincloth (or naked to increase the shame), having been disrobed of His outer tunic and other garments for the flogging of His bare back. About such, Psalm 22:18 reads:

> They divide My garments among them and cast lots
> for My clothing.

This prophecy was fulfilled by the Roman soldiers, as recorded in Luke 23:34:

> And they divided up His clothes by casting lots.

Psalm 31, another psalm of David recording his distress amidst his afflictions, manifests several inferences to the Passion of Christ. For instance, verse 5 states: "Into Your hands I commit My spirit," which were Christ's last words from the cross as recorded in Luke 23:46: "Jesus called out with a loud voice, 'Father, into Your hands I commit My spirit.'" Verses 9–12 describe a man under considerable stress and physical pain who was abandoned by his friends:

> Be merciful to Me, O Lord, for I am in distress; My eyes grow weak with sorrow, My soul and My body with grief.
> My life is consumed by anguish and My years by groaning; My strength fails because of My affliction, and My bones grow weak.
> Because of all My enemies, I am the utter contempt of My neighbors; I am a dread to My friends—those who see Me on the street flee from Me. I am forgotten by them as though I were dead; I have become like broken pottery.

We would be wise to remember that Christ, as this psalm suggests, was abandoned by His disciples in His final hour just as Jesus predicted in Mark 14:27: "You will all fall away." Jesus went on to quote Zechariah 13:7: "Strike the shepherd and the sheep will be scattered."

Psalm 34:20, which states, "He protects all His bones, not one of them will be broken," finds New Testament fulfillment in John 19:36: "These things happened so that the Scripture would be fulfilled: 'Not one of His bones will be broken.'" As will be discussed later, most crucified victims lingered on the cross for 24 to 96 hours before they died. However, Jesus succumbed faster than most crucified victims so that the Roman soldiers did not need to hasten His death by *crucifracture*.[13] Indeed, our sacrificial Lamb, like the lamb or goat in the book of Exodus, had no bones broken in order to fulfill the Scriptures and God's divine plan.

Psalm 41:9 refers historically to David being betrayed by his own relative or close friend, but prophetically points to Judas Iscariot betraying Jesus:

> Even My close friend, whom I trusted, he who shared
> My bread, has lifted up his heel against Me.

Jesus quoted Psalm 41:9 while He was washing the disciples' feet:

> I am not referring to all of you; I know those I have chosen. But this is to fulfill the Scripture: "He who shares My bread has lifted up His heel against Me" (John 13:18).

Psalm 69:21 states: "They put gall in My food and gave Me vinegar for my thirst." Christ was offered drink on two occasions: before being nailed to the cross and immediately before His death. See Mark 15:23. Also, Matthew 27:34 states:

There they offered Jesus wine to drink, mixed with gall;
but after tasting it, He refused to drink it.

Wine or wine mixed with *myrrh* or the bitter substance, *gall*, was sometimes offered to the crucifixion victim in order to dull the senses and ease pain, much like a sedative or narcotic may be given before a medical procedure today.[40]

However, as these verses state, Jesus declined the drink (Matthew 27:34, Mark 15:23); He chose not to avoid fully experiencing the physical pain and anguish that awaited Him on the cross.

Psalm 69:21 also seems to be prophetic of the last moments of Christ's life on the cross, when He was near death and experienced severe thirst due to dehydration and a very dry mouth. During times of dehydration, the brain releases a hormone called *vasopressin* that stimulates thirst. Indeed, as most of us have experienced, thirst can be a very uncomfortable sensation. However, the thirst Christ experienced goes well beyond what we can imagine.

Mark 15:36 states:

One man ran, filled a sponge with wine vinegar, put it on a stick, and offered it to Jesus to drink.

And Luke 23:36 tells us:

The soldiers also came up and mocked Him. They offered Him wine vinegar.

John gives the most detail about Christ's thirst:

Later, knowing that all was now completed, and so that the Scripture would be fulfilled, Jesus said, "I am thirsty." A jar of wine vinegar was there, so they soaked a sponge in it, put the sponge on a stalk of the hyssop plant, and lifted it to Jesus' lips (John 19:28-29).

The Prophets

Isaiah 53, the "suffering servant" chapter, offers perhaps the most graphic and well-known Old Testament prophecy considering Christ's Passion. Isaiah prophesied the coming judgment on the Southern kingdom of Judah during the reigns of Uzziah, Jotham, Ahaz, and Hezekiah. In this context, chapter 53 predicts that the nation of Israel will reject a future servant, who indeed was the coming Messiah. Isaiah describes this coming servant as ordinary and plain in appearance, which led many to overlook Him as having any importance: "He had no beauty or majesty to attract us to Him" (verse 2). In verse 3, this man is described as,

> despised and rejected by men, a man of sorrows, and familiar with suffering...He was despised, and we esteemed Him not.

Some of the most powerful and vivid verses in Scripture pertaining to the crucifixion are found in Isaiah 53. Verse 5 states:

> But He was pierced for our transgressions, He was crushed for our iniquities; the punishment that brought us peace was upon Him, and by His wounds we are healed.

Christ was pierced with nails when He was crucified and after He died His chest was pierced by the tip of a Roman spear. This was performed to ensure His death:

> Because the Jews did not want the bodies left on the crosses during the Sabbath, they asked Pilate to have the legs broken and the bodies taken down.... But when they came to Jesus and found that He was already dead, they did not break His legs. Instead, one of the soldiers pierced Jesus' side with a spear, bringing a sudden flow of blood and water (John 19:31b, 33-34).

Although, at the time, Jesus had already breathed His last:

> Jesus said, "It is finished." With that, He bowed His head and gave up His spirit (John 19:30).

The flow of blood and water has medical significance that will be discussed later.

Peter obviously was familiar with Isaiah 53:5 when he wrote his epistle hundreds of years later. These mortal wounds "heal" us or offer us salvation:

> He Himself bore our sins in His body on the tree, so that we might die to sins and live for righteousness; by His wounds you have been healed (1 Peter 2:24).

Isaiah 53:7 goes on to say:

> He was oppressed and afflicted, yet He did not open His mouth; He was led like a lamb to the slaughter, and as a sheep before her shearers is silent, so He did not open His mouth.

This is borne out in Matthew 26:63 during Jesus' trial before the Sanhedrin: "But Jesus remained silent." Peter later looked back as he wrote his epistle, echoing again the prophet Isaiah:

> When they hurled their insults at Him, He did not retaliate; when He suffered, He made no threats (1 Peter 2:23).

Isaiah 53:8 states:

> For He was cut off from the land of the living; for the transgression of My people He was stricken.

Being cut off from the land of the living refers to death, in Jesus' case, death by crucifixion. This horrendous death Christ suffered, however, was predetermined by God from the foundation of the world (Rev. 13:8), knowing man would sin and need redemption:

> Yet it was the Lord's will to crush Him and cause Him
> to suffer (Isaiah 53:10).

As seen on the night Jesus was in Gethsemane:

> He fell with His face to the ground and prayed, "My
> Father, if it is possible, may this cup be taken from Me.
> Yet not as I will, but as You will" (Matthew 26:39).

Clearly, Isaiah 53 is a powerful section of Scripture that predicts
the suffering of Christ, who was not born until several hundred
years later.

Zechariah 3:8-9 completes the Old Testament references to
Christ's Passion:

> Listen, O high priest Joshua and your associates seated
> before you, who are men symbolic of things to come:
> I am going to bring My servant, the Branch. See, the
> stone I have set in front of Joshua! There are seven eyes
> on that stone, and I will engrave an inscription on it,
> says the LORD Almighty, and I will remove the sin of
> this land in a single day.

These verses refer to "the Branch," the Messiah. The removal of
the sin of the land in a single day may refer to the crucifixion
and death of Jesus.

In addition, Zechariah 12:10 states,

> They will look on Me, the One they have pierced, and
> they will mourn for Him as one mourns for an only
> child, and grieve bitterly for Him as one grieves for a
> firstborn son.

Again, as in Isaiah 53:5, we see the word "pierce" referring
here to the crucifixion of Jesus Christ. "Pierce" connotes an
active, vehement infliction upon someone with a sharp object.

In the case of Jesus, it refers to the spikes or nails piercing His hands (actually the wrists) and feet, as well as the spear inserted into His side after His death.

What a wonderful resource the Old Testament is for Christians to explore not only the Incarnation of God, but also His horrible, selfless, sacrificial death for all of the elect for ages to come.

Praise God!

2

A BRIEF HISTORY

OF

CRUCIFIXION

If a man guilty of a capital offense
is put to death and his body is hung
on a tree, you must not leave his
body on the tree overnight.
Be sure to bury him that same day,
because anyone who is hung on a tree
is under God's curse.

(Deuteronomy 21:22-23)

C RUCIFIXION is an ancient form of capital punishment where-by the victim was tied or nailed to a wooden pole or cross. The Bible alludes to crucifixion in Deuteronomy 21:22-23:

> If a man guilty of a capital offense is put to death and his body is hung on a tree...anyone who is hung on a tree is under God's curse.

However, at this Mosaic time in Jewish history, the victim was usually stoned first and then hung in a tree after death, as a public display of God's and men's curse. The act of crucifixion whereby the accused was attached to a tree, pole, or cross as a means of death was later introduced by non-Jewish culture.[34]

Capital punishment in the ancient world could be very brutal. In fact, the three most barbaric forms of execution are said to be *crux* (Latin: cross, torture; crucifixion), *crematio* (burning alive with fire), and *decollatio* (decapitation).[34] Of these, crucifixion was considered the most brutal. Cicero, a Roman politician and orator, stated that crucifixion was "the most cruel and horrifying death."[10] Crucifixion likely had its origins with the Assyrians and Babylonians. Interestingly, it is these two groups that took the Jews into captivity: the Assyrians overtook the Northern Kingdom (Israel) in 722 B.C. and the Babylonians overtook the Southern Kingdom (Judah) in 605 B.C.[15]

However, crucifixion was probably adopted as a routine means of execution by the Persians in the sixth century, B.C. The Persians, 600 years before Jesus was crucified by the Romans, typically tied the victim to a tree (*infelix lignum*) or impaled him on a vertical post (*crux simplex*).[34] In the book of Ezra, the Persian king Cyrus issued a decree:

> I decree that if anyone changes this edict, a beam is to be pulled from his house and he is to be lifted up and impaled on it (Ezra 6:11).

This brutal punishment of impalement on a pole or post is an example of *crux simplex*. Likewise, in Esther 2, when the Persian king Xerxes heard of an assassination conspiracy planned by two of his royal guards, the king had them impaled on poles, a standard form of crucifixion in ancient Persia. Xerxes' father, king Darius, once executed 3,000 men via impalement on poles, or *crux simplex*.[43] Another example of *crux simplex* impalement is noted in Esther 5 in which Haman and his wife plotted to impale Mordecai on a seventy-five-foot-high stake that would be visible from all directions. Likewise, Jeremiah, in Lamentations 5:12, describes young Jewish exiles being "hung up by their hands," which was likely a primitive form of crucifixion involving impalement or hanging on a wooden stake. Only later in history did crosses utilized for crucifixion take on the shape we consider "traditional" (✝).[4]

Alexander the Great, (356–323 B.C.), the Macedonian king who ushered in the Hellenistic Age, making Greek the universal language of government and literature, supposedly learned about crucifixion from these aforementioned cultures and subsequently introduced crucifixion to the Mediterranean in the fourth century, B.C.[20] Thereafter, crucifixion was learned and implemented in Egypt, Syria, Phoenicia, and Carthage.[13] During the Punic wars between Carthage (an ancient city in North Africa near modern Tunis, Tunisia) and Rome, the Romans learned about the technique of crucifixion and rapidly implemented it as a form of execution.[7] The Romans utilized crucifixion for several hundred years until it was abolished by the emperor Constantine I because of the cruelty of the procedure.[34] The Greeks did not implement crucifixion since they thought it too brutal and inhumane.

THE ROMANS PERFECT THE TECHNIQUE

By the time of Jesus Christ, the Romans were the predominant culture to routinely utilize crucifixion as the primary method of capital punishment. The procedure was mainly reserved for non-Romans, except in special circumstances such as military desertion. The Romans crucified Christians, foreigners, insurrectionists, and slaves. By the time of Christ, Rome was routinely crucifying rebels, mainly Jews. For instance, in 4 B.C., the Romans crucified approximately 2,000 Jews; Josephus, the first-century historian, recorded mass crucifixions that occurred during the Jewish wars, which included persecution under Emperor Tiberius in 19 A.D., the destruction of Jerusalem in 70 A.D. ending the Jewish state, and finally Bar-Kochba's revolt, which failed to restore the Jewish state in 135 A.D.[2, 18, 19]

In first century Palestine, which was occupied by Rome, insurrection against the Roman occupation was common, typically from religious zealots. The Romans killed scores of people for protesting the government, and not all were true criminals such as thieves or murderers. In fact, the allegations against Christ included insurrection and plans to overthrow the Roman government by establishing Himself as King. The religious leaders also accused Him of blasphemy. When Jesus stood before Pilate, the leaders stated: "If He were not a criminal,...we would not have handed Him over to you" (John 18:30). However, the Jewish nation under Rome had no authority to implement capital punishment, so they had to appeal to the Romans; this is why Jesus appeared before Pilate after His conviction by the high priest and the Sanhedrin, the Jewish ruling council.

The Romans continued crucifixion long after Christ died. Josephus notes that during the Roman takeover of Jerusalem in A.D. 70, hundreds of Jewish prisoners were crucified after they rose up against their Roman captors:

> They were first whipped and then tormented with all sorts of tortures before they died, and were crucified before the wall of the city...the soldiers, out of wrath and hatred they bore the Jews, nailed those they caught to the crosses in different postures, by way of jest.[19]

Josephus also recorded a particularly inhumane gesture used by Antiochus IV, in which the victim's strangled child was hung around his neck.[18] These atrocities occurred during the Roman destruction of Jerusalem and the temple in A.D. 70 and were prophesied by Jesus in Luke 23:28-30, while carrying His cross to Golgotha, in response to women along the road who were mourning and weeping for Him:

> Daughters of Jerusalem, do not weep for Me; weep for yourselves and for your children. For the time will come when you will say, "Blessed are the barren women, the wombs that never bore and the breasts that never nursed!" Then they will say to the mountains "Fall on us!" and to the hills, "Cover us."

This prophecy was undoubtedly recalled by those present at the crucifixion when it came to fulfillment approximately thirty-seven years later, as the Roman general Vespasian passed leadership of the siege of Jerusalem in 69 A.D. to his son, Titus, who ransacked and burned the city of Jerusalem. The situation was so grave that mothers saw their sons killed and their corpses piled high in the streets. It is said that starving mothers killed and ate their own babies in order to survive. Christ predicted that this coming Roman invasion would be so horrifying that women would wish that they had not borne children in order to avoid seeing them die terrible deaths. The survivors were sold into slavery if under age seventeen and, if older, were crucified by the thousands all over the Jerusalem landscape. Some have stated that Titus crucified so many people during the A.D. 70 Jerusalem massacre that there was not enough room for all of the crosses and not enough crosses for all of the bodies.

Roman mass crucifixion was also noted by Lucius Anneus Seneca (4 B.C.–65 B.C.):

> I see crosses there, not just of one kind but made in many different ways: some have their victims with their head down to the ground, some impale their private parts, others stretch out their arms.[37]

TECHNICAL ASPECTS OF CRUCIFIXION

As previously noted, the earliest of crucifixions likely involved impaling the victim on a pole (*crux simplex*) or tying him to a tree (*infelix lignum*). By the time the Romans were regularly crucifying people, these early forms were largely abandoned in favor of attaching the person to various types of crosses. The Romans infrequently employed the X-shaped cross (*crux decussata*); most crucifixion victims were attached to the well-known Latin cross (*crux commissa*, in this shape, †) or Tau cross (*crux sublimis*, T-shaped). Tradition holds that Jesus was crucified on the *crux commissa* type of cross. The upright portion of the cross, known as the *stipes*, was implanted permanently in the ground, usually just outside the city in a high-traffic area, so all of the passers-by could witness the horrific event and be deterred from committing crime or insurrection. The horizontal portion of the cross was known as the *patibulum*, and was the section that the victim's wrists were affixed to with rope or, more commonly, iron spikes.[13] The *patibulum* weighed between 100 and 200 pounds and was typically carried over the accused's shoulders to the site of crucifixion, after which it was fastened to the *stipes*, with spikes or rope. At times, a support for the buttocks (*sedile*) was attached to the mid-portion of the *stipes*, although more often omitted since this device afforded the crucified person some relief, which the Romans did not want to provide.

After the victim was found guilty and sentenced to death by crucifixion, a team of Roman soldiers led him in a humiliating procession to the death site.[11] This was done to deter anyone from even contemplating committing the same crime as the accused. The soldier at the head of the procession carried a placard, known as a *titulus*, which bore the victim's name and crime. The soldiers attached the *titulus* to the top of a long wood pole high enough for onlookers to see. The victim was usually stripped at the time of the pre-crucifixion scourging and forced to carry the *patibulum* naked, a tactic aimed at causing further humiliation. Roman law required crucifixion victims to be flogged, or scourged, with whips prior to execution. Only women were exempt. Scourging was meant to weaken—not kill—the victim. However, some victims actually died during the flogging. In addition, the Romans at times employed other forms of torture and maiming such as cutting off the tongue or gouging out the eyes.[34]

After the accused was led to the site and nailed to the *patibu-lum* and erected onto the *stipes*, the Roman centurions presided over the suffering until death occurred, which could take up to three or four days. Sometimes the dead were left on the cross for bugs and vultures to devour. Decomposition in a warm climate would set in quickly, resulting in a putrid odor permeating the vicinity. However, Roman law did allow the family of the dead to remove the corpse and provide proper burial if they so desired. In the case of a Jewish victim, and especially on a Sabbath eve, the body had to be removed before sundown: "You must not leave his body on the tree overnight. Be sure to bury him that same day" (Deuteronomy 21:22). Sometimes, if it was imperative to hasten death, the long bones of the legs were broken, a process known as *crucifracture*.[13] Since the crucified person used his legs to push himself up on the cross in order to breathe, breaking the leg bones (e.g., *femur* and *tibia*) made it impossible for the person to properly inhale and exhale and resulted in rapid asphyxiation and death.

CRUCIFIXION ABOLISHED

Crucifixion was practiced for several centuries before Christ was born and flourished throughout the Roman empire until it was abolished as a form of capital punishment by the first Christian Roman emperor, Constantine I, in A.D. 337.[34] Notwithstanding, countless individuals were executed in this way, not only suffering physical agony but also social scorn and shame. In fact, due to the obscene nature and shame associated with crucifixion, it was a topic not to be discussed in societal gatherings. Cicero noted "This very word 'cross' should be removed not only from the person of a Roman citizen but from his thoughts, his eyes, his ears."[10] We as Christians best remember the curse of crucifixion that Jesus voluntarily submitted to in order to redeem all who would place their faith in Him. The apostle Paul sums it up well in Galatians 3:13:

> Christ redeemed us from the curse of the law by becoming a curse for us, for it is written: "Cursed is everyone who is hung on a tree."

3

GETHSEMANE
AND THE
ALL-NIGHT TRIALS

And being in anguish,
He prayed more earnestly, and His
sweat was like drops of blood
falling to the ground.

(Luke 22:44)

THE night before Jesus was crucified, He met with His disciples for a final Passover meal during which He revealed the symbolic New Covenant:

> While they were eating, Jesus took bread, gave thanks and broke it, and gave it to His disciples saying, "Take and eat; this is My body."
> Then He took the cup, gave thanks and offered it to them, saying, "Drink from it, all of you. This is My blood of the [new] covenant, which is poured out for many for the forgiveness of sins" (Matthew 26:26-28).

Also, Jesus revealed that one who dined with Him at the table that evening would betray Him unto death:

> While they were reclining at the table eating, He said, "I tell you the truth, one of you will betray Me—one who is eating with Me" (Mark 14:18).

This fulfilled the prophecy in Psalm 41:9: "Even My close friend, whom I trusted, he who shared My bread, has lifted up his heel

against Me." This, of course, was Judas Iscariot who betrayed
Jesus for thirty pieces of silver:

> Then one of the Twelve—the one called Judas Iscariot—
> went to the chief priests and asked, "What are you willing
> to give me if I hand Him over to you?" So they counted
> out for him thirty silver coins (Matthew 26:14-15).

Even as this long night was just beginning, Jesus probably
started to experience stress. Long before the crucifixion, Christ
knew that He was going to be crucified:

> Now My heart is troubled, and what shall I say? "Father,
> save Me from this hour"? No, it was for this very reason
> I came to this hour (John 12:27).

> But I, when I am lifted up from the earth, will draw all
> men to Myself (John 12:32).

This foreknowledge about what was to imminently occur, along
with the tension of eating with His betrayer, could have resulted
in scant food intake. Anticipation can lead to many involuntary
physical responses such as *tachycardia* (fast heart rate), nausea,
dizziness, tremor, *diaphoresis* (sweating) and, perhaps, a headache. When one is facing very difficult circumstances, certain
areas of the brain release chemicals called *neurotransmitters*
and the *adrenal glands* secrete hormones such as *cortisol* (i.e.,
cortisone), *epinephrine* (i.e., *adrenaline*), and *norepinephrine*
(i.e., *noradrenaline*). The hormones and chemicals act upon
the heart to cause *tachycardia*; on the sweat glands to cause
sweating; on the blood vessels to cause flushing and dizziness;
and the nervous system to cause headache and tremor. This
involuntary physical condition is known as the "fight or flight"
response and aims to prepare a person to cope with and survive
threatening events. I believe if we could have measured the levels

of the stress hormones *cortisol, norepinephrine,* and *epinephrine* in Jesus' blood at the Last Supper, they would have been very high—in anticipation of horrific things to come.

GETHSEMANE

Following the Last Supper, Jesus and the disciples went to the garden, and Jesus took Peter, James, and John with Him to pray:

> Then Jesus went with His disciples to a place called Gethsemane, and He said to them, "Sit here while I go over there and pray." He took Peter and the two sons of Zebedee along with Him, and He began to be sorrowful and troubled. Then He said to them, "My soul is overwhelmed with sorrow to the point of death. Stay here and keep watch with Me" (Matthew 26:36-38).

Gethsemane is a small garden located on the slopes of the Mount of Olives, just northeast of Jerusalem. The word Gethsemane means "oil press"[43] referring to the pressing of oil from the olive crop. Indeed, Jesus, like an olive, would be squeezed and pressed by the Roman soldiers, and His blood would later seep out of His body like the oil out of an olive when pressed.

As Jesus prayed, His mental anguish was unbearable:

> My soul is overwhelmed with sorrow to the point of death (Mark 14:34).

His deep anguish of soul was no doubt augmented when several times,

> …He returned and found them sleeping. "Could you men not watch with Me for one hour?" He asked Peter. "Watch and pray so that you will not fall into temptation. The spirit is willing, but the body is weak" (Matthew 26:40-41).

He had been betrayed by Judas; and His disciples, who claimed to be followers, had abandoned their watch. Jesus was left to pray alone and wrestle with the enormity of what His Father's will asked of Him. Luke, a physician known for attention to detail, makes a fascinating statement about Jesus' situation in Gethsemane:

> And being in anguish, He prayed more earnestly, and His sweat was like drops of blood falling to the ground (Luke 22:44).

This phenomenon is known as *hematidrosis* and has been reported to occur in situations of intense stress.[13] The capillaries supplying blood to the sweat glands actually break open and leak blood into the sweat ducts, which results in blood being mixed with sweat. This could well have caused severe skin pain due to the underlying inflammation and swelling within the sweat glands. The blood loss, however, would have been scant. In addition, sweating in the cold night air likely caused Jesus to chill and shake which, as we all know, can be quite uncomfortable. Jesus could have had a mild decrease in His body temperature as well (*hypothermia*), especially if there was a breeze. We are also told that Jesus shed tears in the garden, which could have caused redness and irritation of the eyes:

> During the days of Jesus' life on earth, He offered up prayers and petitions with loud cries and tears to the One who could save Him from death…(Hebrews 5:7).

Another physical problem that may have affected Jesus while in Gethsemane was weakness due to poor food and water intake. Remember, during the Passover week Jesus knew of His upcoming betrayal and death and no doubt was troubled. Severe mental stress can cause *anorexia*, or loss of appetite. Jesus' food intake at the Last Supper may have been minimal, and this meal was more about symbolism than eating and satiety. As a result, by the time Jesus reached the garden of Gethsemane, He may have already been mildly dehydrated; and if so, we know that this would have been compounded by fluid loss from His sweating, which in medical terms is called *insensible fluid loss*. Most of us have missed meals for a day or two when ill with a virus. Due to low caloric and fluid intake, low blood pressure (*hypotension*), physical weakness, dizziness, and shakiness can occur, and possibly Jesus was experiencing these that night. Also, if one goes without sufficient food for more than twenty-four hours, the sugar-supplying *glycogen* stores in the liver become depleted and the body burns other fuels called *ketones*, which are formed in the muscles and liver. In my opinion, by the time Jesus reached the garden, He may have already been weak.

A physician can measure what are known as *orthostatic* vital signs: the pulse and blood pressure are measured with the patient lying down and then upright. If the person is dehydrated, the blood pressure will usually fall with standing and the pulse rate will increase. I suspect Jesus would have manifested these vital sign abnormalities at this time, becoming worse over the next several hours.

Another factor to consider regarding Jesus' physical state during the time in Gethsemane is sleep deprivation. Jesus may not have experienced restful sleep during the entire Passover week, and certainly not on the night before the crucifixion, since He was kept awake in all-night trials that started with appearing before the Sanhedrin. Sleep is important for repair and regeneration not only of various organ systems, but also for optimal brain and nervous-system function. When one goes without restful sleep for a few days, weakness, fatigue, nausea, loss of appetite, muscle aches, and headache may occur. Also, responses to fine motor tasks may suffer which could lead to an accident or a fall.

When Judas Iscariot found Jesus on the mountainside, he had with him a large group of armed soldiers. Jesus surrendered Himself voluntarily without resistance: "Am I leading a rebellion, that you have come out with swords and clubs to capture Me?" (Matthew 26:55). Jesus was not treated gently during the arrest, being pushed and shoved around in a harsh manner, which could have resulted in bruising or other minor injuries. So by the time Christ left the garden to appear before the authorities, His physical condition may have already been poor due to physical mistreatment, stress, lack of adequate food and water, fluid loss from sweating, sleep deprivation, and sustaining chills in the night air.

THE TRIALS

Jesus would now face the longest night of His life. He would spend until sunrise being tried for crimes of blasphemy and insurrection, traveling by foot between various places, and ultimately be convicted and sentenced to death by Pilate.

The seventy-one-member Sanhedrin was the Jewish supreme court and consisted of elders, chief priests, and teachers of the law (e.g., scribes and Pharisees). Jesus appeared before Annas, a former high priest and father-in-law of the current high priest. Then He was led to the residence of Caiaphas, whom John wrote of in 18:14, referring to 11:49-53, when, after Jesus raised Lazarus from the dead, they called a meeting of the Sanhedrin:

> Then one of them, named Caiaphas, who was high priest that year, spoke up, "You know nothing at all! You do not realize that it is better for you that one man die for the people than that the whole nation perish."
>
> He did not say this on his own, but as high priest

that year he prophesied that Jesus would die for the Jewish nation, and not only for that nation but also for the scattered children of God, to bring them together and make them one. So from that day on they plotted to take his life.

During these trials, Jesus was accused of blasphemy and many false witnesses appeared: "The chief priests and the whole Sanhedrin were looking for false evidence against Jesus so that they could put Him to death" (Matthew 26:59). To their questioning, "Jesus remained silent" (Matthew 26:63a). They finally found Jesus guilty when the high priest said,

> "I charge you under oath by the living God: Tell us if you are the Christ, the Son of God."
> "Yes, it is as you say," Jesus replied. "But I say to all of you: In the future you will see the Son of Man sitting at the right hand of the Mighty One...." [and]
> Then the high priest tore his clothes and said, "He has spoken blasphemy!" (Matthew 26:63b–65).

The Scripture implies it was unanimous among those present:

> They all condemned him as worthy of death (Mark 14:64b).

and then Jesus was physically and verbally abused, as

> ...some began to spit at Him; they blindfolded Him, struck Him with their fists, and said, "Prophesy!" And the guards took Him and beat Him (Mark 14:65).

This beating should not be confused with the scourging, a fierce flogging upon the bare back and legs with a leather whip. No doubt, the guards were strong and able to inflict very hard blows with their fists, likely causing facial trauma such as lacerations, bruises, black eyes, or even tooth injury; a mild concussion was certainly feasible as well. Indeed, Jesus' face was probably swollen and painful. Job, speaking of himself, said, "My face is red with weeping, deep shadows ring My eyes" (Job 16:16). These dark rings represent stagnated blood around the eye tissues that results from crying, tissue trauma, poor sleep, or overall debilitation—all conditions which may have been afflicting Jesus at this hour.

Furthermore, spitting in one's face was a severe form of degradation during that period of history. Human saliva is also teeming with countless bacteria, which could set the stage for an infection if it came into contact with an open facial injury. By the time Jesus was convicted by the Sanhedrin, His poor physical state had been worsened by these heinous acts. Jesus appeared before the Sanhedrin, Annas, and Caiaphas probably between one in the morning and daybreak, which left Him even more physically exhausted and sleep-deprived. Nonetheless, He did not complain: "He was oppressed and afflicted, yet He did not open His mouth" (Isaiah 53:7). The verbal abuse was also great during this time and added to Jesus' sorrow: "Reckless words pierce like a sword" (Proverbs 12:18).

Under subjugation to Rome, the Jewish rulers did not have the authority execute anyone; only the Roman government could impose the death penalty. Since Pontius Pilate was the Roman procurator over the province of Judea, Jesus was taken before him to hear the case and impose the penalty of death:

> Early in the morning, all the chief priests and the elders
> of the people came to the decision to put Jesus to death.
> They bound Him, led Him away and handed Him over
> to Pilate the governor (Matthew 27:1-2).

Jesus in His weakened and fatigued state had to walk some distance to arrive before the judgment seat of Pilate. Pilate inquired, "What charges are you bringing against this man?" (John 18:29).

When Pilate heard their initial charges, he judged that Jesus' alleged crimes were not worthy of death: "Then Pilate announced to the chief priests and the crowd, 'I find no basis for a charge against this man'" (Luke 23:4). At that point, Pilate referred Jesus to appear before Herod Antipas, the tetrarch of Judah: "When he learned that Jesus was under Herod's jurisdiction, he sent Him to Herod, who was also in Jerusalem at that time" (Luke 23:7). Herod did not pass judgment and sent Jesus back to Pilate for a verdict.

The chief priests kept pressing the issue that Jesus was an insurrectionist trying to set up His own kingdom and, hence, overthrow Caesar. Nonetheless, Pilate still did not believe Jesus worthy of death: "With this he went out again to the Jews and said, 'I find no basis for a charge against Him. But it is your custom for me to release to you one prisoner at the time of the Passover. Do you want me to release the 'King of the Jews'?" (John 18:38-39). Pilate was influenced by the religious leaders' threats to report him to Caesar, with whom Pilate had his troubles,[43] if he did not cave to their wishes and crucify Jesus: "From then on, Pilate tried to set Jesus free, but the Jews kept shouting, 'If you let this man go, you are no friend of Caesar. Anyone who claims to be a king opposes Caesar'" (John 19:12). The people demanded that the murderer and insurrectionist Barabbas be released, in spite of Pilate's pleading on Jesus' behalf:

> All the people answered, "Let His blood be on us and
> on our children!" (Matthew 27:25).

In the end, Pilate gave in (bringing condemnation on himself) and sentenced Jesus:

> Wanting to satisfy the crowd, Pilate released Barabbas
> to them. He had Jesus flogged, and handed Him over
> to be crucified (Mark 15:15).

At this point, remember, the Son of Man had been standing during all of the trials; had traveled by foot to and from the garden and between the locations of Annas, Caiaphas, Pilate, Herod, and back to Pilate; had been awake all night; had not eaten; had been struck and spit on in His face; had been abandoned by most of His Disciples; and had been denied by His close friend, Peter, further adding to His grief. I believe at this point, Jesus would have already been weak and even near collapse, making Him more vulnerable to the next brutal phase of His Passion: the scourging.

4

THE

SCOURGING

*Then Pilate took
Jesus and
had Him flogged.*

(John 19:1)

FLOGGING with a specialized whip, a process known as *scourging*, preceded a Roman crucifixion.[13] Flogging was intended to weaken, but not kill, the victim.

After Jesus was finally sentenced to death, the Roman soldiers led Him to the governor's official residence and judgment hall, in a condescending manner of pomp and circumstance:

> The soldiers led Jesus away into the palace (that is, the *Praetorium*) and called together the whole company of soldiers. They put a purple robe on Him, then twisted together a crown of thorns and set it on Him. And they began to call out to Him, "Hail, king of the Jews!" Again and again they struck Him on the head with a staff and spit on Him. Falling on their knees, they paid homage to Him (Mark 15:16-19).

Romans were quite brutal and demeaning to their condemned. The judge or governor would utter *"Illum duci ad crucem placet,"* which means, "The sentence is that this man should be taken to the cross."[1] The judge then turned to the guards and said,

"*I, miles, expedi crucem*," which translates "Go, soldier, and pre-pare the cross."[31] Scourging, the most brutal and inhumane of punishments, was executed while the cross was being prepared. In the case of Jesus, His humiliation was exacerbated by their mockery. They placed a makeshift royal robe and crown on Him and ridiculed Him by sarcastically paying "homage." Often, when we as humans are physically weakened, we are more vulnerable to external stresses, such as unkind words or daily troubles. Since Jesus was fully human, this ridicule by the soldiers and onlookers only added to His suffering in a time of great physical abuse. Keep in mind how hurtful this must have been, especially as Jesus was grieving over man's fallen condition: "…how often I have longed to gather your children together…but you were not willing!" (Luke 13:34).

Jesus was led to the *Praetorium*, a common meeting place, and this is where His torture intensified. Mark 15:17 notes that after they placed a purple robe on Him, the soldiers "twisted together a crown of thorns, and set it on Him." The crown of thorns may have been more like a wreath or cap that covered Jesus' whole scalp and forehead, and made from a thorny plant indigenous to Palestine called *Paliurus aculeatus*.[28] Pieces of this plant were often dried and kept in containers as kindling to start fires and, hence, were readily accessible. The thorns of this plant are more than an inch long and, when dry, are very stiff and sharp. When this array of thorns was pressed onto Jesus' scalp with force by a soldier, it would have dug deep into Jesus' flesh. In Genesis 3:18, God cursed Adam and Eve because of their sin, sentencing them to toil the earth which "will produce thorns and thistles for you." The growth of thorns, which were a result of man's original sin, became a curse for Jesus as He took upon Himself their sin as well as the sin of all who would trust in Him.

If you have spent time in a garden, you may have experienced being punctured by a rose thorn or a thistle. Significant pain may result and the thorn may become embedded in the skin. Imagine then, a cap with thorns one to two inches long being pressed into your scalp by a firm hand. The thorns became embedded within Jesus' scalp and likely were abutting the skull bone (*calvarium*). There were probably upwards of one hundred thorns on this cap, but this is open to conjecture. Some of the thorns likely broke off within the nerve-laden flesh of the scalp—invoking severe pain.

The human scalp consists of skin, fatty tissue, *fascia* (dense connective tissue), and a specialized tissue attached to the skull called the *galea aponeurotica*. These layers of tissue are no more than a quarter-inch thick. Embedded within the scalp are numerous blood vessels. In fact, the arterial supply of the scalp consists of five branches of arteries derived from the internal and external *carotid* arteries, the major arteries that supply blood to the head and brain. Typically, following a scalp laceration, the vessels do not easily seal off and significant bleeding ensues, until *suture* repair can be performed. Blood can easily dissect between the deep scalp tissue and skull bone and form a *hematoma*, which can later become infected with bacteria. Scalp wounds can bleed so profusely that occasionally a person can bleed to death. Also present within the scalp tissue are numerous branches of sensory nerves which are responsible for pain sensation. For instance, the branches of the sensory-motor *trigeminal* nerve and various *occipital* nerves innervate the scalp and, when irritated with noxious stimuli, result in severe pain.

In Christ's situation, numerous sharp, long thorns would have easily pierced down to the skull, through the *galea aponeurotica*. While cutting through skin and flesh, small arteries (*arterioles*) and veins would have been pierced and significant bleeding would have ensued. The blood likely dripped into His eyes, which may have already been quite irritated from weeping and sweat dripping into them. As a result, it would have been difficult for Jesus to see, not knowing from whom or where the next blow or slap would come. Also, as the thorns passed through the flesh, sensory nerves would have been damaged resulting in unbearable scalp and head pain. It is also quite feasible that Jesus' top eyelids could have been torn by a stray thorn depending how far down the cap or crown was pushed by His persecutor.

By then it was probably seven or eight in the morning on the day of His crucifixion, during Passover Week in the Jewish month of Nisan. Pilate gave the order to have Jesus scourged. Isaiah predicted this event several hundred years earlier: "I offered My back to those who beat Me, My cheeks to those who pulled out My beard; I did not hide My face from mocking and spitting" (Isaiah 50:6). Torture of prisoners was commonplace under Roman rule, and scourging specifically preceded crucifixion. Only women and Roman senators were exempt from pre-execution scourging. Scourging was sometimes called the "halfway death" due to the severe injury it caused, often leaving the victim in a pre-death condition. However, it was known that severe scourging could cause death as well: "When a scourge brings sudden death" (Job 9:23).

Scourging was performed by professionally trained Roman soldiers called *lictors*.[13] It is likely that these men were generally large and strong, which would enable them to inflict serious injury upon their victims. Jesus' hands were bound with ropes and tied around a wooden post, leaving His back fully exposed. The whip was known as a *flagrum*, which consisted of a wooden handle to which were attached several leather thongs.[13] At the ends of these thongs, pieces of metal and jagged animal bones were attached which were intended to dig into and tear through the flesh on the victim's back, buttocks, and thighs. The *lictors* would raise the *flagrum* and put their full force into the action, with the metal and bone fragments striking towards the middle of the back and subsequently leaving an open furrow of flesh, diagonally directed outward toward the side. Psalm 129:3 states: "Plowmen have plowed My back and made their furrows long." And as we saw, Isaiah described Christ's scourging in vivid detail. During the time of scourging, the *lictors* and bystanders taunted Jesus in order to humiliate Him: "They hurl insults, shaking their heads..." (Psalm 22:7) and "All day long My name is constantly blasphemed" (Isaiah 52:5).

It is not clear from Scripture how long Jesus was flogged, although Jewish law limited the lashings to "forty minus one," in order to stay under the legal limit of forty flagellations. This is what Paul referred to when speaking of his own floggings: "Five times I received...forty lashes minus one" (2 Corinthians 11:24). However, Roman law had no such limit, so it may be that Christ received more than that allowed by Jewish law. Two *lictors* performed the scourging, one on each side, and would alternately take turns flogging. The whole of the exposed backside from the nape of the neck to the buttocks bore the brunt of the *flagellum*, but the back of the thighs and calves were targets as well. Some of the *lictors* would flog the victim in the front, striking the abdominal wall, and possibly the genitals, but there is no evidence this was done during Jesus' scourging.

The sharp bones and metal fragments ripped easily through the skin, which consists of the outer layer, or *epidermis*, and the lower layer, or *dermis*. Beneath the skin lies fatty connective tissue, nerves, blood vessels, sweat glands, and hair follicles. Deeper yet, lies a shiny, tough layer called *fascia* that intermingles with the underlying muscle, which is rich in blood vessels.

The sharp pieces of the whip pulled away Jesus' skin and likely penetrated through the deeper tissue layers reaching to the muscles. The major muscles of the exposed back include the *trapezius, latissimus dorsi,* and the rear *deltoid,* or shoulder, muscles. The *latissimus dorsi* muscles are the largest superficial muscles of the back, and are the muscles that are responsible for the "V" shape seen in professional bodybuilders. Deeper back muscles that likely were torn by the *flagellum* include the *rhomboids, spinatus, teres major,* and *serratus posterior.* The large muscle of the buttocks, or *gluteus maximus,* was likely torn as well. Coursing through these muscles of the back are numerous sensory nerves, most of which originate from the spinal nerves of the spinal cord. It is probable that the bone and metal directly tore many of these small sensory nerves resulting in severe, *lancinating* pain. When a nerve is torn, it produces a sharp, searing, and ripping, unbearable sensation—a type of pain referred to as *neuropathic* pain. Imagine hundreds of deep wounds inflicted over the period of a few minutes. The amount of pain associated with this is indescribable and impossible to adequately put into words.

As noted, the back tissue and musculature is rich in blood vessels, most of which originate from the posterior *intercostal* arteries which are branches of the *aorta,* the largest artery in the body. The *intercostal* arteries lie between the ribs and give rise to smaller *arterioles,* like the branches of a tree. It is these branch-like *arterioles* that were ripped open, resulting in profuse bleeding. If the tissue was torn deep enough, the *intercostal* arteries themselves may have been damaged, potentially resulting in profuse blood loss. Numerous small veins were torn as well, which also would have oozed blood. By the end of the scourging process, Jesus' back probably had diagonal stripe-like wounds with dangling skin, fat, and visibly ripped muscles. Human muscle resembles beef, such as steak or roast, in appearance. Jesus' muscles however, would have been shredded and would have more than likely oozed blood, resulting in significant blood loss and a shock-like state.

Multiple rib fractures sometimes occurred due to the severe force inflicted by the *flagellum*. The bone and metal pieces could also tear through the small muscles between the ribs, the *intercostal* muscles, and enter the *thoracic cavity*, causing bleeding into the chest (*hemothorax*) or even causing collapse of the lung (*pneumothorax*). Scripture is definite that none of Jesus' bones were broken, but there is no Scripture to prove it wasn't possible that Christ suffered some of these other complications. It is doubtful His lungs fully collapsed as this would have resulted in rapid death due to inability of the lungs to *oxygenate* the blood. *Contusion* or bruising of the lungs was possible, as sometimes complicates blunt trauma such as that from a car accident or fall. After the scourging, it might have been very difficult for Jesus to breathe due to the severe pain, blood loss, and trauma to the back and *intercostal* muscles. A small *pulmonary contusion*, *hemothorax*, or *pneumothorax* cannot be ruled out, and would have added to Jesus' shortness of breath, a sensation known as *dyspnea*.

One last injury that could potentially complicate scourging would be damage to the kidneys. The kidneys are positioned in the back of the abdominal cavity, an area known as the *retroperitoneum*. The top portion of the kidneys has some protection provided by the rib cage, but the lower part are not afforded such protection and lie basically underneath the layers of back muscles. In fact, it is plausible that during a severe scourging the metal or bone fragments on the *flagrum* could tear through the muscle and dig into the kidney causing significant damage: "Without pity, he pierces My kidneys" (Job 16:13). I suspect Jesus at least suffered contusion to His kidneys which could have resulted in bleeding into the urinary tract, a condition known as *hematuria*. If the bleeding was significant, a clot could have formed within the *ureter* (the tube that connects the kidney to the bladder) and caused obstruction and spasm of the *ureter*, resulting in pain similar to passing a kidney stone (*colic* pain). That people can develop microscopic (invisible) *hematuria* after running or participating in vigorous exercise, leads me to surmise that the significant trauma from the flogging over Jesus' kidneys could have lead to more substantial bleeding, resulting in grossly bloody urine (*gross hematuria*).

Jesus' Condition after Scourging

After the scourging, the soldiers again draped a purple gown on Jesus and taunted Him further: "After they had mocked Him, they took off the robe and put His own clothes on Him. Then they led Him away to crucify Him" (Matthew 27:31). Remember that Jesus' back was an open, swollen, tender heap of exposed bloody flesh. When the robe was pulled off, it may have been stuck to the drying blood and tissue, ripping off shards of skin and muscle, causing intense pain. This added insult to injury, for Jesus was in marginal condition before the flogging even started. After the scourging, Jesus would be considered in critical physical condition if He were admitted to any modern hospital. He had lost a significant amount of blood from the crown of thorns and the scourging. As a result, His pulse was likely elevated (*tachycardia*) and His blood pressure was likely starting to decline (*hypotension*). Shock ensues when a person's blood pressure is too low to provide adequate blood and oxygen to tissues and cells and results in impaired brain function, low body temperature, a faint, thready pulse, poor urine output, and accumulation of acids in the blood, a condition known as *metabolic acidosis.* In addition, the chest trauma and possible lung injury may have resulted in low oxygen levels (*hypoxia*) and inability to fully exhale carbon dioxide (*respiratory acidosis*). Jesus likely manifested all of these findings at the end of the scourging, and although He was conscious, He was not far from death.

In a modern hospital, Jesus in this post-scourging condition would have a battery of laboratory tests and x-rays performed. While not speculating about all of the possible abnormalities and medical scenarios, a few likely conclusions can be drawn to put the Lord's condition into perspective in the context of modern medicine. A chest x-ray would have shown no rib fractures, but possibly fluid within the chest cavity, a condition referred to as a *pleural effusion*. This chest fluid would have contained blood and watery-like fluid. The *sac* around the heart, the *pericardium*, may also have filled with blood and watery-fluid from chest trauma; this has significant physical and spiritual implications that will be discussed in the crucifixion chapter. The collection of fluid and/or blood in this *sac* is called a *pericardial effusion* and may be noted on a chest x-ray or a cardiac ultrasound known as an *echocardiogram*.

Today, Jesus no doubt would have had a computed *tomography* scan ("CT" scan) of His vital organs. Findings on a CT scan would show He had no fractures, but likely have shown bleeding in the chest or abdominal cavities, kidney *contusion*, and swelling of the soft tissues of the chest and back. Routine blood work would show low *hemoglobin* (*anemia*) from bleeding; a low blood pH (*acidosis*) as alluded to earlier; and an abnormal sodium level due to fluid loss from sweating, vomiting, and dehydration. His potassium level may have been elevated from poor kidney function since the kidney regulates potassium balance. A *urinalysis* would show red blood cells in the urine, indicating kidney contusions from the flogging.

Jesus would have been admitted to the intensive care unit (ICU) after the scourging and been given intravenous fluids, oxygen, blood transfusions, and pain control, such as morphine. A surgeon would need to clean out debris in Jesus' back wounds such as dirt, gravel, and wood particles as well as remove dead tissue—a procedure referred to as *debridement*. Antibiotics would be necessary to treat infection which no doubt would be setting in from the unsanitary conditions and the *lictors'* sweat and spittle contaminating the wounds. A *tetanus* shot would be mandatory to prevent *tetanus* or "lockjaw," a deadly infection from bacteria that live in the soil. It is likely that Jesus would have experienced severe respiratory distress necessitating a mechanical ventilator, if He had survived more than a few hours.

Jesus' face was swollen and bloody and His overall appearance was grotesque: "His appearance was so disfigured beyond that of any man and His form marred beyond human likeness" (Isaiah 52:14). Through all of this remember that "by His wounds we are healed" (Isaiah 53:5).

5

THE WALK TO GOLGOTHA

FOOTPRINTS OF JESUS DURING HIS LAST DAYS

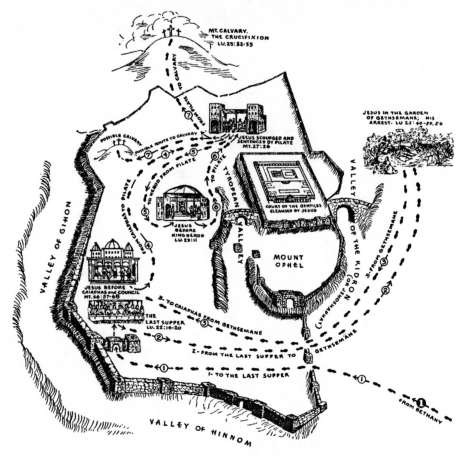

JERUSALEM AT THE TIME OF THE CRUCIFIXION

FOOTPRINTS OF JESUS DURING
HIS LAST DAYS

1. From Bethany to Jerusalem.

   Illustration—In Jerusalem, the Last Supper:
   Lu. 22.14-20.

2. From the Last Supper to the Garden of Gethsemane: Mt. 26.36.

   Illustration—In the Garden of Gethsemane;
   Jesus in Prayer, The Disciples asleep: Lu.
   22.40-50.

3. From Gethsemane to the Palace of the High
   Priest: Mt. 26.57.

   Illustration—Jesus before the Council: Mt.
   26.57-68.

4. From the Palace of Caiaphas to Pontius Pilate's
   Judgment Hall: Lu. 23.1.

5. From Pilate to Herod's Palace: Lu. 23.7.

   Illustration—Jesus before King Herod: Lu.
   23.8-11.

6. From Herod's Palace to Pilate: Lu. 23.11.

   Illustration—In Pilate's Judgment Hall; Jesus
   receiving sentence: Mt. 27.26.

7. From Pilate's Judgment Hall to Golgotha, or
   Calvary: Lu. 23.33.

[See also "Jesus' Hours
upon the Cross," p. 68.]

Taken from the Thompson® Chain-Reference® Bible, p. 1689, and used with permission of Kirkbride Bible Company.

He was oppressed and afflicted,
yet He did not open His mouth;
He was led like a lamb to the slaughter,
and as a sheep before her shearers is silent,
so He did not open His mouth.

(Isaiah 53:7)

AFTER Jesus was flogged, He was led out of the city to the site of crucifixion, a rocky hillside known as Golgotha which, in Aramaic, means "place of the skull." "They came to a place called Golgotha" (Matthew 27:33). Some suggest that this site acquired this name because the rocky crag resembles the profile of a human skull. Others suggest that the name originates from the fact that old skulls from previous crucifixions were scattered on the ground. The Latin term "Calvary" is also occasionally used to refer to this site, which comes from the word *"calvarium,"* another word for skull.[31]

It is noteworthy that Jesus was crucified outside the city gate, a stipulation of Mosaic law in cases of capital punishment: "The man must die. The whole assembly must stone him outside the camp" (Numbers 15:35). In addition, after the high priest performed the blood sacrifice of animals, the bodies were burned outside the camp or city walls: "The high priest carries the blood of animals into the Most Holy Place as a sin offering, but the bodies are burned outside the camp" (Hebrews 13:11). Similarly, Jesus' death and blood-atoning sacrifice took place outside the city walls of Jerusalem: "And so Jesus also suffered outside the city gate to make the people holy through His own blood. Let us, then, go to Him outside the camp, bearing the disgrace He bore" (Hebrews 13:12-13). Essentially, the site of crucifixion was a garbage dump laden with dead animal carcasses and excrement. Crucifying the criminals at this place outside the city was so the many people traveling through the area would see the victims' gruesome punishment and thus be deterred from similar acts.

Jesus Begins the Journey

When Jesus began the trek from the *Praetorium* to Golgotha, He had been awake all night, had had little or no food or water, and was most likely already critically ill from the scourging. Jesus was physically weak and walking anywhere more than a short distance would have been quite difficult and very painful. The typical practice of Roman crucifixion was for the condemned to carry the horizontal portion of the cross, or *patibulum*, across their shoulders and arms.[13] The *patibulum* was tied to the victim, and weighed between 100 and 200 pounds. It is unlikely that the person carried the entire cross, since this would have weighed too much and been too cumbersome to carry any significant distance. The upright portion of the cross, the *stipes*, was often permanently planted in the ground at the crucifixion site. So, Jesus had the *patibulum* affixed to His shoulders and upper back and began the journey. This reminds us of Jesus' comment to His disciples in Matthew 16:24: "Then Jesus said to His disciples, 'If anyone would come after Me, he must deny himself, take up his cross and follow Me.'"

Jesus carrying the wood on His back is reminiscent of Isaac carrying the wood for his own sacrifice up to Mount Moriah: "Abraham took the wood for the burnt offering and placed it on his son Isaac" (Genesis 22:6). God later saved Isaac with a ram in the thicket that provided a substitutionary death, analogous to Christ dying to save His people: "Abraham answered, 'God Himself will provide the lamb...'" (Genesis 22:8).

The typical Roman crucifixion included a procession of the sentenced criminal and Roman centurions. At the head of the procession, a soldier carried a sign known as a *titulus* affixed to a wooden pole. On the *titulus* was inscribed the name and crime of the condemned. At the time of crucifixion, the *titulus* was affixed to the top of the cross, so that those passing by would know the person's name and reason for condemnation. John tells us about Jesus' *titulus*: "Pilate had a notice prepared and fastened to the cross. It read: "JESUS OF NAZARETH, THE KING OF THE JEWS" and "the sign was written in Aramaic, Latin, and Greek..." (John 19:19, 20), so that all who passed by would be able to read it and know who this man was.

THE CROSS IS HARD TO BEAR

Jesus began the approximately half-mile walk to Golgotha in an exhausted and near-shock-like condition. His legs were very weak due to lack of food and from standing during the night trials, walking from place to place, and wounds inflicted during the scourging. Painful wounds on His back and on the back of Jesus' thighs from the scourging made it difficult to walk, let alone carry a large log upon His shoulders. In addition, the *patibulum* was carried on His upper back, in the area of the *trapezius* and upper *latissimus* muscles. The pain of a heavy, rough, splinter-laden piece of wood must have been severe as it rubbed against the gaping wounds.

One may wonder if Jesus' scourge wounds became infected. An infection at this juncture was unlikely since bacteria take a while to proliferate, and infection may take several hours to days to set in. However, some types of *Streptococcus* bacteria and *Clostridium* bacteria can form skin and soft tissue infections within hours, and this may have happened in Jesus' situation. If a soft tissue infection was present, the inflammation and pus formation would have increased the pain to almost incomprehensible levels, making it virtually impossible to shoulder the cross (*patibulum*).

Jesus fell while walking to Golgotha carrying His load, surrounded by a hostile crowd: "But when I stumbled, they gathered in with glee" (Psalm 35:15). For all of the reasons noted in above sections, from a medical perspective it is surprising Christ could walk—even without carrying the wooden beam. Jesus likely had a significant drop in blood pressure (*hypotension*) shortly after embarking on the journey to Calvary. Dehydration, blood loss, severe pain, and stress can result in *hypotension*, especially if one remains in the upright position. When blood pressure drops a significant degree, the brain receives less than adequate blood flow, particularly with blood loss, or *anemia*. Dizziness, light-headedness, or even brief loss of consciousness (*syncope*) may occur to some in this situation. Jesus' injuries could certainly have so weakened His body that He fell to the ground under the great weight of the *patibulum*. It likely was impossible for Him to rise from the ground without having the *patibulum* taken off of His shoulders. Also, as Jesus fell forward, His arms could not brace His fall since they were tied with ropes to the beam. This likely resulted in a full-force fall upon His chest, probably knocking the wind out of Him. A significant blunt force trauma to the breastbone can result in bruising of the heart muscle (*myocardial contusion*). This could result in a fluid collection around Jesus' heart (*pericardial effusion*) which could lead to shock and low blood pressure, if not to death, making it impossible to finish this otherwise relatively short walk.

SIMON OF CYRENE

Jesus had not gone very far when He collapsed under the weight of the *patibulum* and a bystander was seized to carry Jesus' load: "A certain man from Cyrene, Simon, the father of Alexander and Rufus, was passing by on his way in from the country, and they forced him to carry the cross" (Mark 15:21). Cyrene was an ancient city in Northern Africa, located in the vicinity of modern Libya. Many Jews lived there, and no doubt Simon was in Jerusalem for his Passover pilgrimage. He couldn't know at the time, but what Simon was forced to do was recorded in the *Synoptic Gospels*, bearing witness of his deed for ages to come.

6

THE

CRUCIFIXION

JESUS' HOURS UPON THE CROSS

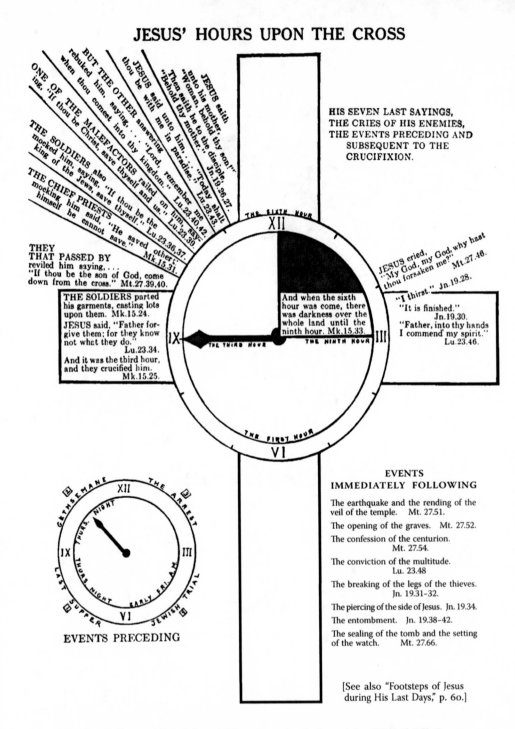

HIS SEVEN LAST SAYINGS,
THE CRIES OF HIS ENEMIES,
THE EVENTS PRECEDING AND
SUBSEQUENT TO THE
CRUCIFIXION.

BUT THE OTHER rebuked him, when thou comest into thy kingdom." Lu.23.40.42.

JESUS said unto him; ... "Today shalt thou be with me in paradise." Lu.23.43.

JESUS saith unto his mother, "Woman, behold thy son!" Then saith he to the disciple, "Behold thy mother." Jn.19.26.27.

ONE OF THE MALEFACTORS railed on him, saying, "If thou be Christ, save thyself and us." Lu.23.39.

THE SOLDIERS also mocked him, saying, "If thou be the king of the Jews, save thyself." Lu.23.36.37.

THE CHIEF PRIESTS mocking him said, "He saved others; himself he cannot save." Mk.15.31.

THEY THAT PASSED BY reviled him saying, ... "If thou be the son of God, come down from the cross." Mt.27.39,40.

THE SOLDIERS parted his garments, casting lots upon them. Mk.15.24.
JESUS said, "Father forgive them: for they know not what they do." Lu.23.34.
And it was the third hour, and they crucified him. Mk.15.25.

And when the sixth hour was come, there was darkness over the whole land until the ninth hour. Mk.15.33.

JESUS cried, "My God, my God, why hast thou forsaken me?" Mt.27.46.

"I thirst." Jn.19.28.

"It is finished." Jn.19.30.
"Father, into thy hands I commend my spirit." Lu.23.46.

EVENTS IMMEDIATELY FOLLOWING

The earthquake and the rending of the veil of the temple.   Mt. 27.51.

The opening of the graves.   Mt. 27.52.

The confession of the centurion.   Mt. 27.54.

The conviction of the multitude.   Lu. 23.48.

The breaking of the legs of the thieves.   Jn. 19.31-32.

The piercing of the side of Jesus. Jn. 19.34.

The entombment.   Jn. 19.38-42.

The sealing of the tomb and the setting of the watch.   Mt. 27.66.

[See also "Footsteps of Jesus during His Last Days," p. 60.]

EVENTS PRECEDING

Taken from the Thompson® Chain-Reference® Bible, p. 1690, and used with permission of Kirkbride Bible Company.

68

And they crucified Him.

(Mark 15:24)

Jesus arrived at Golgotha at approximately nine o'clock in the morning in extremely debilitated physical condition, needing assistance to even stand. Despite this, Jesus would not have had things any other way—willing Himself to die for those who would trust in Him: "He was delivered over to death for our sins" (Romans 4:25). By this time, Jesus had been awake at least twenty-four hours, had minimal food and water, and had been scourged to the point of shock. Upon His arrival at Golgotha, Jesus' garment was ripped from His body, likely tearing and re-opening the bloody wounds on His back. Any clotting of blood that had occurred would have been disrupted by the removal of the tunic which was embedded within the bloody mass of exposed flesh. This would have been very painful. One knows that accidental disruption of a scab is quite painful; Jesus' entire back was one large festering scab-like wound. He was then offered a drink containing *myrrh* (a plant sap with *analgesic* properties) in order to dull the senses prior to crucifixion: "Then they offered Him wine mixed with myrrh, but He did not take it" (Mark 15:23). Certain women who lived in Jerusalem would often offer the crucifixion victim a strong, sedative drink to ease the pain:[1,43] "Give beer to those who are perishing, wine to those who are in anguish; let them drink and forget their poverty and remember their misery no more" (Proverbs 31:6-7). Perhaps Jesus refused the wine and *myrrh* mixture so that He would experience the crucifixion without any clouding of His *sensorium*. Next, Jesus was stripped of His tunic, leaving Him in a small loincloth or naked.[13,34] The soldiers then cast lots for ownership of Jesus' garments, unknowingly fulfilling an Old Testament prophecy: "They divide My garments among them and cast lots for My clothing" (Psalm 22:18).

JESUS IS NAILED TO THE CROSS

The Roman centurions who performed crucifixion were professional executioners who had perfected the technique. The victim was forcefully thrown to the ground, which could have resulted in a concussion. At the very least, however, this was enough to knock the wind out of the victim. This painful act would have caused Jesus' gaping, exposed flesh to become grossly contaminated by soil and gravel if His bare back hit the hard rocky ground. His arms were outstretched onto the *patibulum* and long iron spikes were driven through His wrists into the wood: "The LORD will lay bare His holy arm in sight of all the nations" (Isaiah 52:10). Indeed, people from many nations were present in Jerusalem at this time since it was the pilgrimage of the Passover, and no doubt Jesus' crucifixion was witnessed widely by this diverse group.

Archeological remains of a crucified body found near Jerusalem revealed that the spikes were square and tapered, measuring approximately five to seven inches in length, somewhat resembling a railroad spike.[44] Contrary to popular Renaissance-era sculptures and paintings, I am quite certain the spikes were driven through the wrists and not through the palms, since the weight of the body would have caused the spikes to tear through the hands. One may recite John 20:27 when Jesus appears to Thomas: "Put your finger here; see My hands." The fact that the nails were driven through the wrists, however, is not in contradiction to Scripture, since the wrist and hand were considered one unit in Greek (*cheir*) and the terms were often used interchangeably.[4]

The iron spike passed through the row of wrist bones called the *carpal* bones, sometimes shattering some of these small cube-shaped bones. Nonetheless, the bony structure of the wrist was able to support the weight of the upper body as it hung on the *patibulum*. Minimal blood would be lost in this area since there are no arteries where the spike passed through. However, located in midst of the *carpal* bones in an area known as the *carpal tunnel*, is the large sensory-motor *median* nerve. The *median* nerve supplies motor function to several hand muscles and sensation to much of the hand. The spike, if placed in the center of the palm-side of the wrist, would have pierced or *transected* the *median* nerve, producing severe, burning, *lancinating* pain, a type of discomfort known as *neuropathic* pain. Paralysis of some of the hand muscles would also have occurred. Any subsequent movements of the arms and wrist would result in excruciating pain. Indeed, the word *excruciating* originates from the Latin word *excruciates*, which means "out of the cross." [31,34]

Next, the *patibulum* was attached to the upright post, or *stipes*, which was often permanently planted in the ground at the crucifixion site. The physical jolting as the soldiers moved the *patibulum* to which Jesus was affixed no doubt caused searing pain in the wrist and hands where the spikes were driven. In addition, as Jesus was raised, His back likely rubbed against the rough, splintery wood, further irritating His wounds and forcing wood splinters into the already *friable* tissue: "My back is filled with searing pain; there is no health in My body" (Psalm 38:7). After the *patibulum* was attached to the *stipes* (with rope or spikes), the *titulus* was affixed to the top of the cross on which Pilate had inscribed "JESUS OF NAZARETH, THE KING OF THE JEWS" in Hebrew, Latin, and Greek. Tradition presumes that Jesus was crucified on the †-shaped cross, or *crux commissa*.

Jesus' feet were then nailed to the *stipes* with the same type of iron spike that was driven through the wrists. Most likely, one spike was driven through both feet, as they were overlapped and extended. The ankle joints were probably so extended that the soles of Jesus' feet were parallel to the *stipes*. This degree of non-physiologic *hyperextension* inflicted severe pain, and probably tore some of the ankle ligaments and caused bleeding into the ankle joint (*hemarthrosis*). At the same time, the knees were somewhat flexed to mechanically allow this degree of ankle extension. In any event, the long iron spike passed through the *metatarsal* bones of both feet. Again, as in the hands, no major artery supply runs through the area where the spike was driven. However, it is likely that the spike traumatized nerves, such as deep *peroneal* nerves or the branches of the *medial* and *lateral* *plantar* nerves, which supply innervation and sensation to the foot and sole.

JESUS HANGS

Jesus was crucified mid-morning: "It was the third hour [nine] when they crucified Him" (Mark 15:25). "Two robbers [most often murderers or insurrectionists[13, 19]] were crucified with Him, one on His right and one on His left" (Matthew 27:38).

The weather in Palestine is typically hot and arid, and there was no shade at Golgotha, so the scorching mid-day sun would have been beating down on Jesus' exposed skin. Severe sunburn can occur after one or two hours of direct sun exposure on uncovered skin. Sunburn is an inflammatory reaction of the skin that results from the ultraviolet rays of the sun. If the person remains exposed, severe burn injury can cause painful blisters, often resembling a second-degree burn. I suspect some of Christ's skin experienced a serious and painful sunburn. This would have intensified the pain from the scourging and abrasions He acquired from falling on the road to Golgotha.

In addition to sunburn, another hazard of exposure to a hot, sunny environment is heat exhaustion or, in the most severe form, heat stroke. These conditions result when the body is unable to dissipate heat properly, especially when the person cannot be removed from the hot environment and is dehydrated. This was likely the case with Jesus. As body temperature rises, the skin becomes hot and red, and, eventually, sweating ceases. Sweating is a normal compensatory way that the body tries to cool itself, but with loss of this function, body temperature rises further. Some of the complications of heat illness are intense thirst, headache, kidney failure, disintegration of red blood cells (*hemolysis*), lung injury, and blurred vision. If body temperature rises above 105° F, the person usually becomes delirious and may die. Though Christ probably did not die directly from heatstroke, He very likely had an elevated temperature and symptoms of heat exhaustion, which added to His misery.

While the crucified victim hung exposed and unable to protect himself, insects could land on and burrow into the exposed flesh, or even into the nostrils or ear canals. Since the crucified could not use their hands, it was impossible to deter stinging and biting insects, leaving painful and itchy lesions. Flies may lay eggs into an open wound which could in time hatch into fly larvae, or maggots, resulting in a condition known as *myiasis*. Superimposed infection of the *abraded* skin, known as *cellulitis*, may have occurred, and is commonly due to group *A Streptococcus* (a bacteria which also causes "strep throat" and "flesh eating bacteria" infection) or *Staphylococcus aureus*, a common cause of serious skin and soft-tissue infection. Even in the short time Jesus endured, if infection of Jesus' wounds started to occur, this would have increased the pain of His wounds further and possibly caused a fever, which, in the setting of heat exhaustion, could have raised Jesus' temperature to extreme levels.

COMPLICATIONS OF CRUCIFIXION

Medical, archeological, and historical evidence provides an understanding of some of the specific medical complications that occurred during the crucifixion.

The aim of Roman crucifixion was to cause a very painful, slow, and agonizing death. Victims often survived up to three or four days on the cross, but many died within twenty-four to forty-eight hours. This was not the case with Christ, who survived only approximately six hours. In general, the time the victim survived on the cross was inversely proportional to the degree of injury inflicted during the scourging process. In other words, the more severe the scourging, the shorter time the person survived on the cross. As we have seen, scourging itself was very brutal and injurious and, at times, resulted in death. Jesus' scourging may have been especially severe to coincide with God's providential timing in His dying so quickly.

RESPIRATORY COMPLICATIONS

The major physiologic effect of crucifixion was interference with respiration, or breathing. Normally, inspiration is an active process and exhalation is passive. In other words, it usually takes more work to draw in a breath than to expel a breath, which is more of an involuntary reflex. With a normal inspiration, the *diaphragm* contracts and descends downward toward the abdominal cavity. During expiration, the diaphragm relaxes and ascends. The opposite is true during crucifixion: inhalation becomes passive and expiration is active, requiring an extreme amount of effort. While Jesus hung on the cross, the weight of His body was supported by the wrists. The arms therefore were *hyperextended*, resulting in fixation of the muscles between the ribs (the *intercostal* muscles) in a state of inhalation, thereby interfering with normal passive exhalation. Since exhalation was impaired, air would become trapped within the lungs, a state known as *hyperinflation*. In this condition, the lungs could not adequately expel carbon dioxide, leading to *respiratory acidosis*. Patients with *respiratory acidosis* eventually experience a drop in blood pH, normally about 7.4. As the level of Jesus' blood pH fell, muscle cramps and contractions known as *tetany* probably occurred, further inhibiting expiration.

In order to breathe, the crucified person would passively take a breath while hanging with his arms extended. To exhale, the elbows and shoulders would need to be forcefully moved in order to pull oneself up toward the top of the cross. As the wrists moved during this process, the spike irritated the *median* nerve causing bouts of electric-shock-like pain not only at the wrist, but also radiating up the arms toward the shoulders and neck. Jesus' shoulders may have dislocated, making it unbearably painful to move them in any manner. However, Jesus likely did not have the strength to pull His body up. He needed to push His body upwards with the legs, with the entire weight of His body pushing against the *metatarsal* bones of the feet where the spike was driven. This causes *lancinating* pain in the foot and ankle with each expiration. Also, as Jesus raised Himself up to exhale, the raw, seeping, tender, exposed tissues on His back would scrape against the splintery wood of the vertical *stipes*, adding another element to the pain. Most victims could survive for hours to a few days like this, repeating the awfully painful procedure of raising the body up to complete the respiratory cycle. This came at a horrible price, resulting in severe pain at the spike sites and upon the back. This must have been a pitiful sight to behold.

Other respiratory problems encountered during crucifixion could include *aspiration* and coughing. As the victim hung, oral secretions and an irritated, dry throat likely led to coughing fits. In fact, we are told Jesus had a dry mouth: "Later, knowing that all was now completed, and so that the Scripture would be fulfilled, Jesus said, 'I am thirsty'" (John 19:28). It is quite likely that the throat muscles were weak, making it difficult to *expectorate* secretions. Weakened throat muscles could make the crucified victim prone to *aspirating* oral contents into the lungs.

Jesus likely vomited while on the cross. Patients with severe trauma and pain often experience reflex nausea and vomiting, an active process causing contraction of several muscles within the torso. If Christ vomited, His uncontrollable body movements would have caused the open, festering wounds on His back to move forcefully against the cross, making this an extremely painful ordeal. If oral contents or *vomitus* migrates into the *trachea* and lungs, inflammation of lung tissue occurs, a condition known as *aspiration pneumonitis*. This can lead to coughing, chest discomfort, shortness of breath, and low oxygen levels. If Jesus *aspirated*, this would have made His breathing all the more difficult.

Compounding this, the collection of watery fluid within the chest cavity, called a *pleural effusion*, would have added a burden to Christ's breathing. *Pleural effusion* is significant, since John 19:34 refers to "blood and water" flowing from Jesus' side when the centurion pierced His chest with a spear. It is likely that the water was *pleural* fluid since the spear entering the chest cavity caused a sudden rush of fluid out of the spear wound.

If a crucifixion was taking too long, death could be hastened by breaking the victim's legs. This brutal procedure, known as *crucifracture,* typically involved a Roman soldier applying an intense, blunt force to the lower extremities with a club or rod, although axes were occasionally used.[13,34] The *femur* (thigh bone) and the *tibia* (shin bone) are very strong, hard bones in an average man and require severe force to break. This pain inflicted on a dying person is beyond description. Once the legs were broken, the crucified person could not push up on the cross to exhale. As a result, rapid increase in carbon dioxide levels and lowering of blood oxygen would result in *asphyxiation* and horrific death within a few minutes.

In the case of Jesus and the two thieves, it was a religious necessity for them to be dead and removed from the crosses before sundown because of the impending Sabbath:

> Now it was the day of Preparation, and the next day was to be a special Sabbath. Because the Jews did not want the bodies left on the crosses during the Sabbath, they asked Pilate to have the legs broken and the bodies taken down. The soldiers therefore came and broke the legs of the first man who had been crucified with Jesus, and then those of the other. But when they came to Jesus and found that He was already dead, they did not break His legs (John 19:31-33).

The soldiers were unknowingly fulfilling the Old Testament prophetic model concerning the treatment of the sacrificial Passover lamb in Exodus and Numbers, and the prophecy in Psalm 34:20.

One additional respiratory problem Jesus may have experienced is a *pulmonary embolism*, or a blood clot in the blood vessels of the lungs. These clots almost always travel from the leg veins through the heart and lodge in the vessels of the lungs known as the *pulmonary arteries*. This is not an infrequent complication that occurs in hospitalized patients who are bedfast. *Pulmonary embolism* can kill immediately, or more likely lead to chest pain, shortness of breath, or coughing up blood (*hemoptysis*).

Jesus would have been at very high risk for forming blood clots in His leg veins (*venous thrombosis*) since He had undergone physical trauma and was very dehydrated, which increases the risk of this complication. If Jesus had *venous thrombosis* in the leg, *pulmonary embolism* could occur, making breathing all the more difficult. *Hemorrhage* into lung tissue can complicate *pulmonary embolism* as well as *thoracic trauma, aspiration pneumonitis*, and critical illness, resulting in *hemoptysis*. Coughing up blood is an alarming occurrence, not only to the patient, but also to onlookers. Jesus may have coughed up blood as He hung on the cross and some could have spilled onto those up close —soldiers, family, and friends.

HEART COMPLICATIONS

Heart, or *cardiac*, problems affected Jesus as He hung on the cross. By this time, we know Jesus lost a significant amount of blood, was increasingly dehydrated and in severe pain. All of these problems lead to an increased heart rate (*tachycardia*) and low blood pressure (*hypotension*). In some cases, if dehydration is severe or if there is a very low red blood count (*anemia*), severe stress on the heart can occur, a process known as high-output *congestive heart failure*. The lungs can fill up with fluid, causing severe shortness of breath. Also, from the scourging trauma and from Jesus' fall as He carried the *patibulum*, it is likely He sustained chest-wall injury and possibly damage to the heart muscle *(myocardial contusion)*. This can lead to collection of fluid or blood within the *pericardium*, the small *sac* that encases the heart. If this fluid collection is large, it is known as a *pericardial effusion* and can result in low blood pressure, heart failure, and shock. We have no way of knowing if Jesus had a *pericardial effusion*, but today a test called an *echocardiogram* could diagnose this condition. If present, however, it would have added to Jesus' weakened condition and likely hastened His demise.

Christ likely had a *pericardial effusion* filled with blood based on John's observation: "Instead, one of the soldiers pierced Jesus' side with a spear, bringing a sudden flow of blood and water" (John 19:34). It is likely that the water John witnessed was the fluid around the lungs, a *pleural effusion*, first encountered by the spear tip. Subsequently, this was followed by the spear piercing the *pericardium*, then resulting in a flow of bloody fluid, a bloody *pericardial effusion*. As the spear punctured the heart muscle, blood flowed out of the wound.

Again, Scripture was fulfilled: "They will look on Me, the One they have pierced" (Zechariah 12:10). Lamentations 3:13 states: "He pierced My heart with arrows from his quiver," which may even foreshadow the lance piercing Jesus' chest resulting in the flow of blood and water.

Perhaps this is what the elderly, righteous Jew, Simeon, who was waiting for the Messiah, meant when he told Mary and Joseph regarding their son when they brought Him to the temple on the eighth day:

> This child is destined to cause the falling and rising of many in Israel, and to be a sign that will be spoken against, so that the thoughts of many hearts will be revealed. And a sword will pierce your own soul too (Luke 2:34-35).

MISCELLANEOUS COMPLICATIONS

This study is not meant to be a technically exhaustive medical treatise of crucifixion, but instead a concise, understandable narrative and summary of Christ's sufferings. As such, it covers the most likely and relevant medical complications in a readable manner. However, other miscellaneous medical problems Jesus could have experienced as a direct result of crucifixion are worth noting.

From a general *metabolic* standpoint, Jesus' body temperature was probably elevated, likely exceeding 100° F. Since Jesus was dehydrated from little oral intake and much sweating, vomiting, and blood loss, He probably had an elevated sodium level in His blood (*hypernatremia*). This condition occurs when people lose salt-rich fluid and cannot replenish the losses with water or other liquids, and the sodium level rises. Most people know sodium as a component of table salt, or sodium chloride. But sodium is one of the most abundant metals in the body, and the level may change significantly with losses of fluid or dehydration. Severe, unquenchable thirst is also invariable when one has a high sodium level and results from the brain's release of *anti-diuretic hormone*. We have all experienced thirst on a hot day, but imagine this sensation compounded several times. Also, when dehydration is very severe, as in the case with Jesus by this point in time, the kidneys may not receive adequate blood flow, which can lead to kidney failure. Urine output may decrease and toxins such as *urea* (an ammonia-containing compound) can build up in the blood, leading to nausea, vomiting, weakness, headache, and, if untreated, coma. Jesus died before coma set in, but He may have exhibited these other symptoms of kidney failure and undoubtedly severe dehydration. Blood potassium levels may increase in this setting as well, which can cause muscle cramps, weakness, and sometimes abnormal heart rhythms (*arrhythmia*).

As Jesus became more critically ill, His *metabolism* began to burn fuels other than *glucose* and *glycogen*, a sugar which is stored in the liver. This would have made Him prone to *hypoglycemia*, or low blood sugar, with symptoms of dizziness, weakness, and headache. Eventually, the body burns other fuels, resulting in what is called *anaerobic metabolism*. This leads to an excess accumulation of acid in the blood, or *metabolic acidosis*, which can lead to heart dysfunction, increased potassium levels, and eventually shock and death. Most systems of the body do not operate normally during severe *metabolic acidosis*. Near the end of His life, Jesus likely had a significant *metabolic acidosis*.

Infection of Jesus' wounds could have started to set in as well. Remember, He had open back wounds from the scourging, thorns digging into His scalp, and nails, probably dirty and rusty, piercing His wrists and ankles. He had been spit upon, and since saliva contains millions of bacteria, this may have infected His wounds. While *tetanus* would not have occurred in this short time period, other bacterial infections were certainly plausible. The bacteria *Streptococcus* and *Staphylococcus* can invoke a rapidly spreading infection of the skin and soft tissue known as *necrotizing fasciitis*. *Clostridium* bacteria can induce a rapidly fatal soft-tissue infection known as *gas gangrene*, which typically develops in *devitalized* wounds grossly contaminated with dirt, as with Jesus. It is feasible that Christ was developing a skin infection or even a deeper infection within the exposed flesh (*abscess*). Both of these infections in a normal person can be life-threatening, much more so in Jesus' condition. If this were the case, fever, chills, and worsening pain would occur, again adding to our Lord's suffering.

CONCLUSION

Jesus was fully human and had a body anatomically and physiologically identical to ours that was just as susceptible to injury and illness: "The Word became flesh..." (John 1:14a). He experienced extreme thirst (John 19:28), pain (Isaiah 53:10), and intense anguish (Matthew 26:38). Jesus felt upon His shoulders the weight of all the sin of fallen mankind and the wrath of His Holy Father, causing Him excruciating grief: "My God, My God, why have You forsaken Me?" (Mark 15:34). Jesus experienced sorrow, temptation, and bodily pain just as we mortal, broken vessels when we suffer:

> For we do not have a high priest who is unable to sympathize with our weaknesses, but we have One who has been tempted in every way, just as we are—yet was without sin (Hebrews 4:15).

7

HIS

DEATH

Into Your hands
I commit My spirit.

(Psalm 31:5)

JESUS was crucified at approximately nine in the morning, and died six hours later, at approximately three in the afternoon. Most crucified individuals survived for more than six hours, with some victims suffering for up to four days. Crucifixion was not intended to result in a rapid, convenient death, but rather was meant to impose prolonged, intense agony and despair. So why did Jesus die in such a short time period? Both criminals flanking Jesus had their legs broken to hasten death before sundown on this Sabbath eve (John 19:32-33). Why was it that Jesus was already dead and did not require *crucifracture*? Although many have put forth theories as to the immediate cause of Jesus' death, it is worth noting Jesus' medical condition during His final minutes up until He ultimately gave up the ghost.

THE END OF A LONG DAY

Jesus' physical stresses initially began the night before in Gethsemane when He literally was sweating blood (*hematidrosis*). There, He was manhandled by a large band of armed soldiers and led to the trials before the Sanhedrin and high priest where He was punched, spat upon, and pushed down. He had no sleep during this period and was not fed or provided adequate liquids. After appearing before the Sanhedrin and high priest, Jesus was taken to Pilate, then to Herod, and back again to Pilate where He was finally sentenced. This ordeal went on all night through the early morning hours and Jesus had to walk to the different destinations. Finally, Jesus was handed the death penalty and scourged until He was critically ill. In fact, He was too weak to carry the *patibulum* to Golgotha, and Simon of Cyrene was enlisted to complete this task. Upon arrival to Calvary, Jesus was pale, covered with large, seeping, painful bloody wounds upon His back, buttocks, and legs, and had a swollen face from the thorny crown and other abuse from the soldiers. His eyes were probably almost swollen shut, making it difficult to see. I also suspect He could not walk under His own power and had to be supported by the soldiers as He made the trek.

As described in detail earlier, by this point Jesus was very ill and in great physical pain, yet "He did not open His mouth" (Isaiah 53:7). We probably would have shuddered in horror to see Him:

> Just as there were many who were appalled at Him—
> His appearance was so disfigured beyond that of any
> man and His form marred beyond human likeness"
> (Isaiah 52:14).

He was a swollen bloody mess in excruciating pain and, if admitted to an emergency room today, would be swarmed by medical personnel for urgent and dire diagnostic testing and treatment. But He had yet to finish and fulfill His ultimate purpose: to voluntarily suffer and die by crucifixion as the sacrifice for sin:

> He was crushed for our iniquities; the punishment that
> brought us peace was upon Him, and by His wounds we
> are healed . . . the LORD has laid on Him the iniquity
> of us all (Isaiah 53:5b, 6b).

He was now at the pinnacle of God's eternal, sovereign plan. He faced his final moments abandoned and in physical agony. His closest friends, with the exception of John [generally accepted as *the disciple whom Jesus loved*], had run away in fear: "Strike the shepherd, and the sheep will be scattered…" (Zechariah 13:7b).

THE NINTH HOUR

In Palestine, time was stated by hours, with six in the morning representing the first hour of the day. We are told in Scripture that from the sixth hour (noon) until the ninth hour (three in the afternoon), the sun ceased to give light: "At the sixth hour darkness came over the whole land until the ninth hour" (Mark 15:33). During this time, Jesus was approaching death and God sent a phenomenon of darkness in the midst of day, which signified the darkness of sin that Christ was bearing at His time of death.

Jesus made a last-minute arrangement with the apostle John to care for His mother Mary:

> When Jesus saw His mother there, and the disciple whom He loved standing nearby, He said to His mother, "Dear woman, here is your son," and to the disciple, "Here is your mother" (John 19:26-27).

From a physiologic standpoint, it was very difficult for Jesus to speak—He probably uttered single words, taking deep breaths between each word. Speaking occurs during exhalation and was an active, painful, energy-consuming process for a crucified victim. Air from the lungs is pushed out with the contraction of the diaphragm and other muscles, and passes through the vocal cords, which vibrate and subsequently produce sound. The amount of effort it took for Jesus to speak any words, let alone sentences, was significant and required extraordinary energy expenditure. Jesus would have needed to push Himself up in order to speak, an excruciating process.

Shortly after this, John records the following: "Later, knowing that all was now completed, and so that the Scripture would be fulfilled, Jesus said, 'I am thirsty'" (John 19:28). This statement fulfilled Psalm 22:15: "and My tongue sticks to the roof of My mouth" and Psalm 69:21: "They put gall in My food and gave Me vinegar for My thirst." Indeed, the prophet Jeremiah noted his own suffering which seems to parallel Christ's maladies at this time in history: "I remember My affliction and My wandering, the bitterness and the gall" (Lamentations 3:19). Jesus was offered a drink of vinegar, which He accepted:

> A jar of wine vinegar was there, so they soaked a sponge in it, put the sponge on a stalk of the hyssop plant, and lifted it to Jesus' lips. When He had received the drink, Jesus said, "It is finished." With that, He bowed His head and gave up His spirit (John 19:29-30).

Luke notes that this occurred at about the ninth hour (three in the afternoon) when: "Jesus called out with a loud voice, 'Father, into Your hands I commit My spirit.' When He had said this, He breathed His last" (Luke 23:46). This was in fulfillment of Psalm 31:5: "Into Your hands, I commit My spirit."

JESUS DIES

Jesus died only six hours after being nailed to the cross, a rather rapid death for crucifixion. "Pilate was surprised to hear that He was already dead. Summoning the centurion, he asked him if Jesus had already died. When he learned from the centurion that it was so, he released the body to Joseph" (Mark 15:44-45). This is a significant statement from Pilate who, no doubt, was involved with many crucifixions and knew that most victims survived for a much longer time.

Why did Jesus die more rapidly than most crucified individuals? Mysteries abound in God's Word. Men "put Jesus to death" (Acts 2:23), yet could not take His life. Jesus with His mere command raised the dead and decayed body of Lazarus to a fully restored body and life. Neither could death take Jesus. Yet His physical condition corresponds to His giving up His life for our sake. Physically, Jesus' quick death was likely in part related to the severity of the scourging, which without question left Him in shock and critically ill. When a person is already ill, any subsequent physical trauma is poorly tolerated. For instance, if an individual is critically ill from *pneumonia* and has poorly controlled *diabetes* and *congestive heart failure*, a new problem such as a *stroke* may not be tolerated and prove fatal. In other words, the body is generally less able to withstand new illness or injury in the face of underlying critical illness. This is precisely the situation that faced Jesus. By the time He reached Golgotha, He was critically ill. The further physical trauma of crucifixion compounded His already weakened condition.

It is evident that severe anguish plagued Christ during His Passion: "He offered up prayers and petitions with loud cries and tears..." (Hebrews 5:7). Furthermore, it is known that with severe stress the body mounts a hormonal response, releasing *adrenaline* and similar compounds that stimulate various body systems including the *cardiovascular* and immune system. Normally, this response is meant to help protect the individual in times of moderate stress, such as fear or physical danger. However, in a situation of extended and intense stress and danger, the body may *maladapt* to this normally beneficial hormonal response, causing increased work for the heart and weakening of the immune system. This very response created by God to protect us, may have, in an extreme form, hastened Jesus' body reaching fatal condition.

Remember, Jesus was carrying the holy wrath of His Father against sin—what could have been heavier to bear?

Victims of crucifixion often survived longer on the cross, even several days. However, this was not in God's will for Jesus, since the bodies of those crucified that Sabbath eve needed to be removed before sundown, in keeping with Jewish law. If Jesus were alive at sundown, His legs would have been broken just as the criminals' were, in order to cause rapid death by *asphyxiation*. But this would have violated Old Testament prophecy in Psalm 34:20. Jesus was indeed the ultimate Passover lamb.

Many medical writers and physicians have offered various theories as to what may have been the physical conditions of Jesus at death. One theory is that Jesus died of a *myocardial rupture*, or a "broken heart." This theory postulates that when Jesus fell carrying the *patibulum* on the way to Golgotha, He sustained severe blunt chest trauma because, falling forward with His arms not free to break His fall, Jesus would have struck His chest squarely on the stony path, resulting in bruising of the heart muscle, known as a *myocardial contusion*. Subsequently, some suggest that the bruised, weakened heart muscle ruptured due to the severe stress placed upon the heart. This, of course, would result in sudden, rapid death. This is not such a plausible explanation for Jesus' death, because it typically takes a few days after a trauma for the heart muscle to "soften" enough to rupture, a rare complication of a massive heart attack. In such a rare case, several days after a major heart attack the area of dead, softened heart muscle can rupture and lead to a sudden, catastrophic death. So while it is possible Jesus died of *myocardial rupture*, it is unlikely due to the short time.

Another frequently offered analysis of Christ's physical conditions at death was a collection of fluid and blood in the *sac* around the heart, the *pericardium*. If enough fluid collects, especially in a rapid fashion, this can impede the heart's ability to pump blood, with shock and death following unless the fluid could be quickly drained with a needle (*pericardiocentesis*). Jesus may have had a *pericardial effusion* from the scourging and the fall on the road to Golgotha. This remains a very plausible explanation of His physical condition and may be supported by the outpouring of "blood and water" noted in John 19:34, when Jesus was lanced by the centurion's spear, a maneuver performed in order to ensure death. The water represented fluid in the chest cavity and the blood likely emanated from the *pericardial sac* from prior chest trauma. In any event, there is no question that Jesus was dead at this time, which should silence any who believe Jesus was only unconscious when removed from the cross.

Jesus knew by the prophecies at what time He would die:

> ...He said to His disciples, "As you know, the Passover is two days away—and the Son of Man will be handed over to be crucified" (Matthew 26:1b-2).

Mark 15:37 states, "With a loud cry, Jesus breathed His last." Physically, this may have been a shriek from a sudden jolt of severe pain or from relaxation of Jesus' chest and abdominal musculature, causing a sudden outflow of air. If the vocal cords were closed, this could result in a groaning sound due to the turbulence of air rushing out of the lungs.

However, Luke and John both record that He spoke. When in God's providential timing He knew the overwhelming weight of His Father's wrath had reached its climax and been satisfied (verse 19:28), Jesus said,

> "It is finished" (John 19:30b);

> And the curtain of the temple was torn in two. Jesus called out with a loud voice, "Father, into Your hands

I commit My spirit." When He had said this, He breathed His last (Luke 23:46b).

For since death came through a man, the resurrection of the dead comes also through a man. For as in Adam all die, so in Christ all will be made alive (1 Corinthians 15:21-22).

. . . because He suffered death, so that by the grace of God He might taste death for everyone (Hebrews 2:9b).

...our Savior, Christ Jesus, who has destroyed death and has brought life and immortality to light through the gospel (2 Timothy 1:10b).

A TWENTY-FIRST CENTURY EXPLANATION OF JESUS' CONDITION AT DEATH

Other alternative explanations of Jesus' fatal condition are possible. If Jesus could have been examined by a physician just before death, He would have been *obtunded* or almost unconscious when He uttered His final words, "Father into your hands I commit My spirit" (Luke 23:46). Also, His pulse would have been rapid, weak, and *thready*, and His blood pressure would be very difficult, if not impossible, to detect with a blood pressure cuff and stethoscope. His skin would have been clammy and His fingers and toes would likely have exhibited a bluish tinge known as *cyanosis*, which results from poor blood flow and low oxygen levels. His respiratory effort would have been labored, but very shallow, not allowing adequate intake of oxygen and expiration of carbon dioxide. He may also have exhibited increased oozing of blood at the nail sites, scalp, mouth, and from the crucifixion and scourging wounds. A phenomenon known as *disseminated intravascular coagulation* (DIC) frequently occurs in critically ill patients and results in diffuse bleeding from disruption of the blood clotting system.

In summary, a multitude of physical problems including blood loss, infected wounds, low oxygen and high carbon dioxide levels from poor respiratory mechanics, severe dehydration, and perhaps kidney failure contributed to the destruction of Jesus' body. Overall, when a person has a prolonged period of low blood pressure and low oxygen levels, the cells and tissues cannot operate normally. The *metabolism* of the cells is altered and a substance called *lactic acid* is produced, resulting in a condition known as *metabolic acidosis*. In this setting, the acidity of the blood increases, resulting in a lowering of blood pH. Normal blood pH is 7.4 and the body operates well only within a very narrow range of blood pH (7.35–7.45). Once the acid level in the blood increases and the pH drops below approximately 7.1 or 7.0, the function of all of the cells within the body is severely disrupted. This includes the muscle cells of the heart, the *neurons* of the brain, and blood cells, to name a few. As the pH drops, the body cannot adequately keep blood potassium levels normal, and the potassium level in the bloodstream rises to dangerous levels, a condition known as *hyperkalemia*. The danger of *hyperkalemia* is a heart *arrhythmia* known as *ventricular fibrillation*, which is invariably fatal if left untreated. In addition, *metabolic acidosis* in and of itself can lead to severe shock and heart dysfunction, and death if not immediately treated.

Jesus' possible critical conditions at death were multiple. By the ninth hour, Jesus likely had a significant *metabolic acidosis* and a high potassium level in His bloodstream. This situation would be compounded by the rising carbon dioxide levels that would have occurred as Jesus became too weak to push Himself up on the cross to exhale. This buildup of carbon dioxide results in what is known as *respiratory acidosis*, which also causes the pH of the blood to drop and become more acidic. The pH of Jesus' blood was probably very low, likely less than 7.0, a level that is not conducive to supporting function of multiple organs, especially the *brain* and *heart*. As the *acidosis* worsened, Jesus may have drifted in and out of semi-consciousness and experienced a problem with electrical activity of the heart resulting in an *arrhythmia* or cardiac standstill, known as *asystole*.

Any physician who cares for the critically ill can often tell by just simple visual observation if a patient's death is imminent. If experienced physicians had been present toward the end of the crucifixion of Jesus, their assessment would have been that Jesus was going to die very soon and not linger like many crucified victims.

WAS JESUS REALLY DEAD?

Over the years, critics and skeptics of Christianity have put forth the idea that Jesus did not really die, but was only unconscious when removed from the cross. They state that when Jesus was placed in the tomb, He was merely unconscious from dehydration and fatigue, only to reawaken later and exit the tomb under His own power. This is at odds with Scripture and medical science. As noted above, the centurion verified to Pilate that Jesus was dead: "When he learned from the centurion that it was so, he gave the body to Joseph" (Mark 15:45). John records in his Gospel that the soldiers were certain Jesus was dead: "But when they came to Jesus and found that He was already dead, they did not break His legs" (John 19:33). Is it possible that the soldiers were mistaken and that Jesus was still alive? Absolutely not! Remember, these soldiers were professional executioners who performed crucifixion routinely. They knew their job and they knew it well enough to know when a person was dead. In addition, the thrust of the spear into Jesus' chest would inflict mortal injuries that would be incompatible with life.

Other evidence that Jesus was unquestionably dead is revealed in several passages about Jesus' burial within the tomb that Joseph of Arimathea provided for Christ's body. This tomb was carved out of a massive rock and had a large stone placed in front to seal the opening, as Matthew 27:59-60 attests:

> Joseph took the body, wrapped it in a clean linen cloth, and placed it in his own new tomb that he had cut out of the rock. He rolled a big stone in front of the entrance to the tomb and went away.

Mark 15:46 tells us that Joseph "took down the body, wrapped it in the linen, and placed it in a tomb cut out of rock." To remove a dead body from a cross was no small feat. I am not sure how much Jesus weighed but even if He weighed only 150 pounds, it would have taken at least two or three people to remove His body from the cross and carry Him to the tomb. Anyone who has carried "dead weight" can attest to the difficulty of this. The point is that if Jesus were alive, it would have been evident to one of Jesus' followers as they removed the nails and physically manipulated and moved Christ's body. They would have noticed breathing and movements of the eyes, chest wall, or limbs. Therefore, it is impossible that Jesus was alive when taken off the cross, and, of course, Scripture fully supports this view.

Jesus was placed in a tomb newly hewn out of rock. Matthew 27:66 states: "So they went and made the tomb secure by putting a seal on the stone and posting the guard." The large heavy stone was rolled down a slope in a groove that was meant to keep the stone securely in place. It would have been impossible for Jesus if He were alive and in a weakened state to move a stone that weighed at least several hundred pounds. Furthermore, the stone was sealed, likely with cord and wax, and heavily guarded at the entrance, and breaking this seal from within by a critically ill man would have been impossible. In addition, Jesus' face was wrapped in burial cloth per the local tradition of the region. This impinging cloth secured over the mouth and nose, in conjunction with a sealed-up tomb, would have caused rapid suffocation—even if Jesus were alive (which is impossible). Therefore, it is not feasible from logical medical analysis that Jesus was alive, let alone able to exit the tomb under His own power. The only plausible explanation is that Christ was dead and nothing but a supernatural, miraculous event—the Resurrection—could bring Him back to life and remove the stone while guarded by armed soldiers.

> There was a violent earthquake, for an angel of the
> Lord came down from Heaven and, going to the tomb,

A first century tomb, from outside and inside, showing the groove and round stone for sealing. Photos by Desta Garrett, Israel, 1995.

rolled back the stone and sat on it. His appearance was like lightning, and his clothes were white as snow. The guards were so afraid of him that they shook and became like dead men.

The angel said to the women, "Do not be afraid for I know that you are looking for Jesus, who was crucified. He is not here; He has risen, just as He said. Come and see the place where He lay. Then go quickly and tell His disciples: 'He has risen from the dead...'"

When the chief priests had met with the elders and devised a plan, they gave the soldiers a large sum of money, telling them, "You are to say, 'His disciples came during the night and stole Him away while we were asleep.' If this report gets to the governor, we will satisfy him and keep you out of trouble." So the soldiers took the money and did as they were instructed. And this story has been widely circulated among the Jews to this very day. (Matthew 28:2-7a, 12-15)

JESUS' RESURRECTION DEFEATS ETERNAL DEATH

Jesus died and on the third day rose again, fulfilling numerous Old Testament prophecies:

For what I received I passed on to you as of first importance: that Christ died for our sins according to the Scriptures, that He was buried, that He was raised on the third day according to the Scriptures...
(1 Corinthians 15:3-4).

His voluntary shedding of blood established and sealed the New Covenant, fulfilling the Old Covenant which was unable to save and sanctify. Christ's one-time death satisfied the universal requirement of death for sin against a holy God: "Because by one sacrifice He has made perfect forever those who are being made holy" (Hebrews 10:14), and made the duty of executing the ritual Law to the letter and the sacrifice of animals obsolete. His death and resurrection have overcome death which entered with Adam's fall, renewing our old death-destined self to newness in Him, to culminate in eternal life. Christ died once and conquered death so that it has no mastery over Him nor those who have placed their trust in His atoning blood:

> If we have been united with Him like this in His death, we will certainly also be united with Him in His resurrection. For we know that our old self was crucified with Him so that the body of sin might be done away with, that we should no longer be slaves to sin—because anyone who has died has been freed from sin. Now if we died with Christ, we believe that we will also live with Him. For we know that since Christ was raised from the dead, He cannot die again; death no longer has mastery over Him (Romans 6:5-9).

Jesus' resurrection crushed Satan's plan to destroy mankind, as alluded to in Genesis 3:15: "He will crush your head, and you will strike His heel." Despite Satan's attempt to bruise Jesus through the crucifixion, it was Satan who was defeated through Christ's resurrection. Indeed, Satan is the father of earthly evil but Jesus' death and resurrection foiled Satan's attempt to condemn mortals to eternal death:

> Since the children have flesh and blood, He too shared in their humanity so that by His death He might destroy him who holds the power of death—that is, the devil— and free those who all their lives were held in slavery by their fear of death (Hebrews 2:14-15).

If we as humans are honest, death frightens and perplexes most of us. Let's face it: nobody wants to think about his own demise.

A question I have been asked many times by dying patients not wanting to experience discomfort is, "Will it come with pain or physical suffering?" Even as a physician, death still remains a mystery to me. From a medical standpoint, the heart ceases to pump blood and the lungs fail to transmit oxygen into the bloodstream. As a result, all cells of the body die—from the *brain* to the *bicep*. Shortly thereafter, cellular mechanisms fail and the blood stagnates within the veins. The immune system cannot ward off bacterial contamination and the intestinal wall breaks down, spilling billions of bacteria throughout the system. These bacteria and a lack of oxygen lead to tissue decay, known as *necrosis*. The foul odor of death is the result of *putrifying* bacteria that consume all of the person's tissues, thereby releasing chemicals (e.g., sulfur compounds and a chemical known as *putrecine*) that lead to the severe stench if the body is not immediately cooled, embalmed, or buried: "Their dead bodies will send up a stench" (Isaiah 34:3). Mary and Martha were concerned that when their brother Lazarus' tomb was opened there would be an overwhelming odor: "'But Lord,' said Martha, the sister of the dead man, 'by this time there is a bad odor, for he has been there four days.'" (John 11:39). We all know that Jesus performed a great miracle that day, raising Lazarus from the dead with no trace of decay or stench of death.

The lack of bodily decay in Lazarus was a foretaste of Christ overcoming death: "Because You will not abandon Me to the grave, nor will You let Your Holy One see decay" (Psalm 16:10). Jesus' resurrection means that eternal death was defeated for believers and, along with it, freed "those who all their lives were held in slavery by their fear of death" (Hebrews 2:15b).

Yes, our dead, mortal bodies will rot and decay, eventually returning to the dust of the earth: "By the sweat of your brow you will eat your food until you return to the ground, since from it you were taken; for dust you are and to dust you will return" (Genesis 3:19). Even though we all will die because of the deeds of the first Adam, we have hope for eternal life without decay through the resurrection of the second Adam, that is, Jesus Christ: "For as in Adam all die, so in Christ all will be made alive" (1 Corinthians 15:22). Despite the fact that one day our cells will cease to function and bacteria will invade our flesh, the life of Jesus will pervade believers for eternity:

> We always carry around in our body the death of Jesus, so that the life of Jesus may also be revealed in our body. For we who are alive are always being given over to death for Jesus' sake, so that His life may be revealed in our mortal body (2 Corinthians 4:10-11).

Jesus Himself shed light on the cause of His death, when he said, in John 10:15b, 17-18:

> I lay down my life for the sheep.... The reason my Father loves me is that I lay down my life—only to take it up again. No one takes it from me, but I lay it down of my own accord. I have authority to lay it down and authority to take it up again. This command I received from my Father.

The true cause of Jesus' death is that—although man cannot save Himself,

> God so loved the world that He gave His one and only Son, that whoever believes in Him shall not perish but have eternal life (John 3:16).

8

WHAT DOES ALL THIS MEAN FOR ME?

For He bore the sin of many,
and made intercession
for the transgressors.

(Isaiah 53:12)

JESUS CHRIST was tortured beyond belief and suffered an agonizing death and was buried, fulfilling the Scriptures. He exemplified the epitome of the humble, suffering servant attitude, which we as believers are to emulate as Paul outlines in Philippians 2:5-8:

> Your attitude should be the same as that of Christ Jesus: Who, being in very nature God, did not consider equality with God something to be grasped, but made Himself nothing, taking the very nature of a servant, being made in human likeness. And being found in appearance as a man, He humbled Himself and became obedient to death—even death on a cross!

So what? Should not the real focus be on the resurrection, which many churches celebrate as Easter Sunday, and the crucifixion acknowledged, but down played, because of the violence? After all, we have enough violence and gore in today's society with assault, murder, accidents, and natural disasters. In light of this, why do we need to focus more on the crucifixion? Should we just mention the crucifixion in passing to our children but not discuss it in detail lest we frighten them? Should we as mature believers only talk about the crucifixion superficially, and then only on the Passion Week day we annually commemorate it? The real crux of Christianity is what happened on Resurrection Day, when Jesus conquered death. So why not just skim over the details of Christ's death and focus on other more comfortable topics? I hope to help us appreciate why the crucifixion was and still is an important event for believers to contemplate, like Paul:

> I want to know Christ and the power of His resurrection and the fellowship of sharing in His sufferings, becoming like Him in His death, and so, somehow, to attain to the resurrection from the dead (Philippians 3:10-11).

Indeed the commemoration Jesus instructed us to observe is Holy Communion, (Luke 22:19-20):

> And He took bread, gave thanks and broke it, and gave it to them, saying, "This is my body given for you; do this in remembrance of me." In the same way, after the supper He took the cup, saying "This cup is the new covenant in my blood which is poured out for you...."

> ...whenever you eat this bread and drink this cup, you proclaim the Lord's death until He comes (1 Cor. 11:26b).

Remembering the crucifixion will help us see Jesus' resurrection as even more glorious and, hopefully, enhance our walk with Christ.

FOR THE SKEPTIC

Skeptics exist today just as they did in Jesus' day. Perhaps the best known skeptic of Jesus' resurrection was Thomas, one of the twelve disciples. Thomas spent three years walking with and learning from Jesus and was present at the Last Supper. He had heard Jesus refer to His coming death and subsequent rising from the dead, although this was a difficult concept for all of the disciples to grasp. Nonetheless, this disciple has become known as "doubting Thomas" due to his famous statement: "Unless I see the nail marks in His hands and put my finger where the nails were, and put my hand into His side, I will not believe it" (John 20:25). Despite this emphatic proclamation, Jesus, in grace and love, met Thomas in a manner appropriate to his personal condition and understanding, as we see in John 20:26-29:

> A week later His disciples were in the house again, and Thomas was with them. Though the doors were locked, Jesus came and stood among them and said, "Peace be with you!" Then He said to Thomas, "Put your finger here; see My hands. Reach out your hand and put it into My side. Stop doubting and believe." Thomas said to Him, "My Lord and My God!" Then Jesus told him, "Because you have seen Me, you have believed; blessed are those who have not seen and yet have believed."

Even today, Jesus will reach out and meet those of us, skeptics included, who are willing to place their faith in Him.

When Jesus died, He died in the flesh. His body became pale as well as cold and stiff (*rigor mortis*) just like all of our bodies will one day. This was because Jesus was fully God, incarnate in flesh, fully human, living with the human race, who are finite, temporal beings created in His own image: "The Word became flesh and made His dwelling among us" (John 1:14). In order to save us, He had to become a human being, take on Himself—though sinless—our sin including the alienation from God our sin causes, suffer bodily abuse and excruciating pain, and die a physical death like each of us, to pay our deserved death penalty. Jesus, however, rose from the dead bodily, not in the form of a spirit, but in the flesh, being fully alive, yet transformed, as foreshadowed in His transfiguration on the mountain (Matthew 17:1-9). There were those who did not recognize Him after the resurrection, even though He was physically in their midst. Consider those walking to Emmaus, who talked with Jesus about the recent events, but did not recognize Him until their eyes were opened (Luke 24:13-35).

Jesus' resurrected body was as physically real as it had been for the previous thirty-three years of His life. The two who walked on the Emmaus road and did not initially believe, realized this when they ate with Jesus: "Then the two told what had happened on the way, and how Jesus was recognized by them when He broke the bread" (Luke 24:35). Later, Jesus appeared to the eleven disciples in a divinely transformed yet real body:

> While they were still talking about this, Jesus Himself stood among them and said to them, "Peace be with you." They were startled and frightened, thinking they saw a ghost. He said to them, "Why are you troubled, and why do doubts rise in your minds? Look at My hands and My feet. It is I Myself! Touch Me and see; a ghost does not have flesh and bones, as you see I have." When He had said this, He showed them His hands and feet. And while they still did not believe it because of joy and amazement, He asked them, "Do you have anything here to eat?" They gave Him a piece of broiled fish, and He took it and ate it in their presence (Luke 24:36-43).

Again, we see Christ revealing Himself to the disciples who, despite spending three years with Him, were still skeptical. In His desire to make Himself real to all, He met each of them in a personal way to jar their skepticism into solid, unyielding belief. He still does that for us today—even the skeptics.

Jesus rose in a spiritually transformed physical body, not a ghostly, ethereal one like an apparition that could not be touched or felt. In the above passage, the disciples witnessed Jesus' body and wounds and saw He was a real breathing man (yet divine) with skin, flesh, and bones. The fact that Jesus ate a piece of broiled fish proves that He had the anatomy of a real human man—He had teeth to chew the food and a stomach to receive it. An apparition would not and could not eat. Another example of the resurrected Christ exhibiting His physical body is found in Acts 1:3-4: "After His suffering, He showed Himself to these men...over a period of forty days and spoke about the kingdom of God. On one occasion, while He was eating with them...." This passage confirms that Jesus rose in bodily form and should silence any skeptic.

JESUS DIED FOR ALL

From the beginning of time, God destined His Son to come to earth: "He was chosen before the creation of the world" (1 Peter 1:20a); and die: "...the Lamb that was slain from the creation of the world" (Revelation 13:8); in order to save mankind: "He suffered death, so that by the grace of God He might taste death for everyone" (Hebrews 2:9).

Jesus' reason for entering our world as a baby and living a completely righteous life was to ultimately die on the cross in order to redeem mankind from the plague of sin:

> For you know that it was not with perishable things such as silver or gold that you were redeemed...but with the precious blood of Christ, a lamb without blemish or defect. He was chosen before the creation of the world" (1 Peter 1:18-20a).

This remains a mystery that God in His infinite wisdom had ordained His coming to us as a man to die, even before the creation of the world. When mankind fell into sin (Genesis 3), the only thing that could redeem Adam and his sons was the death of the second Adam (Jesus Christ) and faith that He rose from the dead. Ironically, Jesus died upon a tree, a part of His own creation (Genesis 1:11) that would later serve as the vehicle of His death:

> He Himself bore our sins in His body on the tree, so that we might die to sins and live for righteousness; by His wounds you have been healed" (1 Peter 2:24).

Christians are saved by His blood as the sacrificial lamb who died once and for all. The duty of the high priest to enter the tabernacle with the blood of an unblemished lamb each year on the day of Atonement was suddenly dissolved when Christ died. In fact, when Jesus died, the veil shrouding the Most Holy Place where the presence of God was manifest was torn, as noted in Mark 15:38: "The curtain of the temple was torn in two from top to bottom." The fact that it was torn from top to bottom signifies that God above tore it, allowing man to enter into God's presence through the Son of Man, Son of God, Jesus, thus eliminating the need for a human intercessor like the high priest to offer animal sacrifices. After all, Jesus Christ is the great High Priest:

> Now there have been many of those priests, since death prevented them from continuing in office; but because Jesus lives forever, He has a permanent priesthood. Therefore He is able to save completely those who come to God through Him because He always lives to intercede for them (Hebrews 7:23-25).

SAVED BY BLOOD AND WATER

The apostle John, who witnessed Jesus' death, writes in 1 John 5:6: "This is the one who came by water and blood—Jesus Christ. He did not come by water only but by water and blood." Blood sacrifice was and still is necessary for salvation.

In the Old Testament, the lamb's blood on the lintel and sides of the doorframes saved the Israelites from the Angel of Death (Exodus 12:22-23).

The New Covenant, however, through the shedding of Christ's blood, replaced the need for animal sacrifice once and for all. Paul eloquently summarizes this New Covenant centered on Christ's blood sacrifice in Ephesians 1:7-8:

> In Him we have redemption through His blood, the forgiveness of sins, in accordance with the riches of God's grace that He lavished on us with all wisdom and understanding.

The significance of water in 1 John 5:6 refers to baptism, but in the context of crucifixion, as noted earlier that when the spear was thrust into Jesus' chest, out poured water and blood. Physiologically, this water was *pleural* or *pericardial fluid* from severe injury and stress. But this water has more significance since John, who was an eyewitness, mentioned it in his Gospel: "Instead, one of the soldiers pierced Jesus' side with a spear, bringing a sudden flow of blood and water" (John 19:34). This flow of blood and water made a lasting impression upon John when he wrote First John many years later as an older, introspective, and Holy Spirit inspired man. He had time to reflect on the sacrifice Jesus made when he alluded to the literal and spiritual blood and water in 1 John 5:6. Jesus indeed is the Rock who was literally split physically and poured out water for our salvation: "He split the rock and water gushed out" (Isaiah 48:21).

CONCLUSION

Contemplating the crucifixion of Jesus Christ can make us uncomfortable. We do not like to discuss the specifics and avoid talking about the graphic details in recent movies on the subject.

Mark A. Marinella, M.D.

When we consider in detail the horrific nature of His sacrifice, however, we quickly realize that Jesus underwent unspeakable anguish and physical pain—unlike what most humans ever have to endure. Many of us only think about the crucifixion during the Passover season, and only then on a superficial level, glossing over the details of what really happened to our Savior during His final days on this earth. The thought that Christianity is supposed to make us feel good is a misconception. Contemplating Christ's sacrifice and His suffering the scourge-induced grotesque bloody wounds, the cap of long thorns piercing His scalp, and the long iron spikes piercing His wrists and ankles shakes us. Reflecting on Jesus' voluntary sacrifice and physical pain enables us to grasp the fact that Jesus Christ was fully human with a body no different from ours. He felt pain, hunger, and thirst just as we do. He was the Son of Man filled with the Holy Spirit and the Son of God incarnate in flesh. He was and is the living, breathing Word of God (John 1:1), who willingly experienced the ultimate in physical torture because He desired above all else to save His people from sin and death and give hope to all mankind. This is the crux of Christianity, integral to a proper understanding of the Gospel. Paul sums up Christ's sacrifice succinctly in Colossians 2:13b-14:

> He forgave us all our sins, having canceled the written code, with its regulations, that was against us and that stood opposed to us; He took it away, nailing it to the cross.

You see, not only was Jesus' body nailed to that plank of rough-hewn wood, but also the Law, which could not save mankind. Not only did the nails hold Jesus and the Law to the cross, but my sins (and yours) did as well.

Think about it.

APPENDIX

In Christ Alone

In Christ alone my hope is found;
He is my light, my strength, my song;
This cornerstone, this solid ground,
Firm through the fiercest drought and storm.
What heights of love, what depths of peace,
When fears are stilled, when strivings cease!
My comforter, my all in all—
Here in the love of Christ I stand.

In Christ alone, Who took on flesh,
Fullness of God in helpless babe!
This gift of love and righteousness,
Scorned by the ones He came to save.
Till on that cross as Jesus died,
The wrath of God was satisfied;
For ev'ry sin on Him was laid—
Here in the death of Christ I live.

There in the ground His body lay,
Light of the world by darkness slain;
Then bursting forth in glorious day,
Up from the grave He rose again!
And as He stands in victory,
Sin's curse has lost its grip on me;
For I am His and He is mine—
Bought with the precious blood of Christ.

No guilt in life, no fear in death—
This is the pow'r of Christ in me;
From life's first cry to final breath,
Jesus commands my destiny.

No pow'r of hell, no scheme of man,
Can ever pluck me from His hand;
Till He returns or calls me home—
Here in the pow'r of Christ I'll stand.

Words and Music by Keith Getty & Stuart Townend

WHEN I SURVEY THE WONDROUS CROSS

When I survey the wondrous cross
On which the Prince of Glory died,
My richest gain I count but loss,
And pour contempt on all my pride.

Forbid it, Lord, that I should boast,
Save in the death of Christ, my God;
All the vain things that charm me most,
I sacrifice them to His blood.

See, from His head, His hands, His feet,
Sorrow and love flow mingled down;
Did e'er such love and sorrow meet,
Or thorns compose so rich a crown?

Were the whole realm of nature mine,
That were a present far too small;
Love so amazing, so divine,
Demands my soul, my life, my all.

Isaac Watts (1707)

BIBLIOGRAPHIC REFERENCES

1 Andrews, S. J. *The Life of Our Lord upon the Earth*. 4th Ed. NY: Charles Scribner and Company, 1868, [73, 529, 536].

2 Ausubel, Nathan. *Pictorial History of the Jewish People*. NY: Crown Publishers, Inc., 1953.

3 Ball, D. A. "The Crucifixion and Death of a Man Called Jesus." *Journal of the Mississippi State Medical Association*, 1989, [30:77-83].

4 Barbet, P. *Doctor at Calvary: The Passion of Our Lord Jesus Christ as Described by a Surgeon*. Trans., Earl of Wicklow. Garden City, NY: Doubleday Image Books, 1953, [12-18].

5 Barclay, W. *The Gospel of Mark*. Louisville, KY: Westminster John Knox Press, 1975.

6 Barclay, W. *The Gospel of John*, Vol. 1. Philadelphia: The Westminster Press, 1975.

7 Boatright, M. T., D. J. Gargola, and R. J. A. Tilbert. *A Brief History of the Romans*. NY: Oxford University Press, 2006, [59-67].

8 Bishop, J. *The Day Christ Died*. NY: Harper and Brothers, 1957.

9 Bourne, F. C. *A History of the Romans*. Boston: D. C. Heath and Company, 1966.

10 Cicero. *Pro Rabirio*. Trans. H. D. Hodge. Loeb Classical Library. Cambridge, MA: Harvard University Press, 1927.

11 DeBoer, S. L. and C. L. Maddow. "Emergency Care of the Crucifixion Victim." *Accident and Emergency Nursing*, 2002, [20:235-239].

12 Dinsmore, M.H. *What Really Happened When Christ Died.* Denver: Accent Books, 1979.

13 Edwards, W.D., W.J. Gabel, and F.E. Hosmer. "On the Physical Death of Jesus Christ." *Journal of the American Medical Association,* 1986, [255:1455-1463].

14 Fleetwood, J. *The Life of Our Blessed Lord and Saviour Jesus Christ: and the Lives and Sufferings of the Holy Apostles and Evangelists.* Chicago: American Mutual Library Association, 1890.

15 Friedrich G. *Theological Dictionary of the New Testament.* G. Bremiley, Ed. Trans. Grand Rapids, MI: W.B. Eerdmans, 1971, [7:572-73].

16 Holoubek, J.E. and A.B. Holoubek. "Execution by Crucifixion: History, Methods and Cause of Death." *Journal of Medicine,* 1995, [26:1-16].

17 Hume, B. *The Mystery of the Cross.* Brewster, MA: Paraclete Press, 1998.

18 Josephus. *Jewish Antiquities.* Trans. L.H. Feldman. Loeb Classical Library. Cambridge, MA: Harvard University Press, 1981, [XII:256].

19 Josephus. *Jewish War.* Trans. H. St.J. Thackeray. Loeb Classical Library. Cambridge, MA: Harvard University Press, 1957, [III: 321; V: 362-420].

20 *Lincoln Library of Essential Information.* Buffalo, NY: The Frontier Press, 1964.

21 MacArthur, J. *Hard to Believe.* Nashville, TN: Thomas Nelson Publishers, 2003.

22 MacArthur, J. *The Murder of Jesus.* Nashville, TN: Thomas Nelson Publishers, 2004.

23 Manning, Brennan. *A Glimpse of Jesus.* NY: HarperCollins Publishers, 2003.

24 Marinella, M. A. *Frequently Overlooked Diagnoses in Acute Care.* Philadelphia, PA: Hanley and Belfus, 2003.

25 Marinella, M. A. *Recognizing Clinical Patterns: Clues to a Timely Diagnosis.* Philadelphia, PA: Hanley and Belfus, 2002.

26 Marinella, M. A. "Maggot Infestation of a Chronic Leg Ulcer." *Infections in Medicine,* 2004, [21:268].

27 Maslen, M. W. and P. D. Mitchell. "Medical Theories on the Cause of Death in Crucifixion." *Journal of the Royal Society of Medicine,* 2006, [99:185-188].

28 Moore, David M., Ed. *The Marshall Cavendish Illustrated Encyclopedia of Plants and Earth Sciences,* Vol. 2. NY: Marshall Cavendish, 1988, [258].

29 Mould, E. W. K. *Essentials of Bible History.* NY: Thomas Nelson and Sons, 1939.

30 Netter, F. H. *Atlas of Human Anatomy.* 2nd Ed. East Hanover, NJ: Novartis, 1997.

31 *Oxford Latin Dictionary.* Ed. James Morwood. Oxford, England: Oxford University Press, 2005, [417].

32 Porter, A. M. "The Crucifixion." *Journal of the Royal Colleges of Physicians of London,* 1991, [25:271].

33 Porter, J. R. *Jesus Christ: The Jesus of History, The Christ of Faith.* NY: Oxford University Press, 1999.

34 Retief, F. P. and L. Cilliers. "The History and Pathology of Crucifixion." *South African Medical Journal,* 2003, [93:938-941].

35 Riggs, R. M. *The Life of Christ.* Springfield, MO: Gospel Publishing House, 1968.

36 Rutland, M. *Resurrection: Receiving and Releasing God's
   Greatest Miracle.* Lake Mary, FL: Creation House Publishing,
   2005.

37 Seneca, L. A. In *De Consolation ad Marciam,* Ed. H. C.
   Michaelis. Harlem, NY: Vincent Loosjes, 1840.

38 Spurgeon, Charles Haddon. *The Treasury of David.* Volume 1.
   NY: Funk and Wagnalls, 1882.

39 Strauss, L. *The Day God Died.* Grand Rapids, MI: Zondervan
   Publishing House, 1965.

40 Stroud, W. *Treatise on the Physical Cause of the Death of
   Christ and Its relation to the Principles and Practice of
   Christianity,* 2nd Ed. London: Hamilton and Adams, 1871,
   [28-156, 489, 494].

41 Tenney, S. M. "On Death by Crucifixion." *American Heart
   Journal,* 1964, [68:286-287].

42 Tintinalli, J. E., G. D. Kelen, and J. S. Stapczynski. *Emergency
   Medicine: A Comprehensive Study Guide.* 5th Ed. NY:
   McGraw-Hill, 2000.

43 Walvoord, J. F. and R. B. Zuck. *The Bible Knowledge Com-
   mentary: Old Testament.* Colorado Springs, CO: Cook
   Communications Ministries, 2004, [87, 188].

44 Zias, J. and E. Sekeles. *The Crucified Man from Giv'at ha-
   Mivtar: A Reappraisal.* Israel: Explor J, 1985, [35:22-27].

MARK A. MARINELLA, M.D.

ABOUT THE AUTHOR

Dr. Marinella is a perfect candidate to author this book. Having completed his Bachelor of Science at Mount Union College in Alliance, Ohio, he earned his M.D. and became a Fellow in Medical Oncology at Wright State University School of Medicine in Dayton, Ohio. He trained in internal medicine at the University of Michigan Medical Center in Ann Arbor, Michigan, and is currently practicing medical oncology in Dayton, Ohio. He is certified by the American Board of Internal Medicine and is a fellow of the American College of Physicians (F.A.C.P.). Between his internal medicine training and beginning his study of oncology, Dr. Marinella spent more than ten years as a "hospitalist" (hospital-based general internist). He went on to master human physiology while caring for thousands of patients and teaching medical students and internal-medicine residents on a daily basis. During this time, he was an active member of his local church.

Dr. Marinella has authored four books, five book chapters, and more than 100 published manuscripts in medical literature.

Steven D. Burdette, M.D.

ACKNOWLEDGMENTS

I N addition to my Savior who has given me the ability to think and write, I wish to thank my friends and colleagues, Steven D. Burdette, M.D. and Wendy G. Schmitz, M.D., for their thoughtful medical expertise in reviewing the manuscript.

Also, thanks to Steven D. Burdette, M.D. for his contribution of the "Foreword" and "About the Author."

Likewise, my appreciation goes to Rev. Christopher Hoops for initial theological analysis of the manuscript, and editor Mark Kakkuri, who contributed editing to the manuscript and ideas for an introduction.

I also extend my deepest thanks to Rev. David Snowden, Stephen Julian, PH.D., Rev. Pete Schwalm, Rev. Douglas Peters, David K. Smith, D.D., and Dennis Sullivan, M.D. for their support and constructive feedback.

I also wish to extend my appreciation for final production to Desta Garrett, editor and book designer; Ron Kirk, theological editor, who reviewed the Scripture citations; Kimberley Winters, proofreader; Robbie Destocki, cover designer; and Jerry Nordskog, publisher, for believing in this work and making this book a reality.

Most of all, I am forever indebted to Rebecca, my wife, who has shown me grace, patience, and unyielding encouragement, even when I did not realize or deserve it.

Mark A. Marinella, M.D.

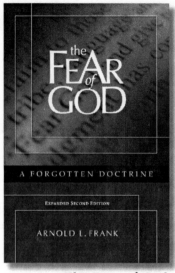

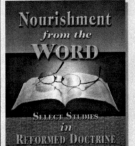

Printed in the United States
134557LV00002B/2/P